Children at Play

Children at Play

§

Using Waldorf Principles
to Foster Childhood Development

Heidi Britz-Crecelius

Park Street Press
Rochester, Vermont

Park Street Press
One Park Street
Rochester, Vermont 05767

Translated by Christian and Ingrid von Arnim from the second German edition
(1972).

Originally published in German under the title *Kinderspiel—lebensentschiedend* by
Verlag Urachhaus in 1970.

LIBRARY OF CONGRESS CATALOGING-IN-PUBLICATION DATA
Britz-Crecelius, Heidi, 1920–
    [Kinderspiel lebensentscheidend. English]
    Children at play : using Waldorf principles to foster childhood
development / Heidi Britz-Crecelius.
    p. cm.
    Originally published: New York : Inner Traditions International, 1986.
    Includes bibliographical references.
    ISBN 0-89281-629-5
    1. Play—Psychological aspects. 2. Child development. I. Title.
BF717.B7513 1996   96-4205
155.4'18—dc20   CIP

Printed and bound in the United States

10 9 8 7 6 5 4 3 2 1

This book was typeset in Bembo

Park Street Press is a division of Inner Traditions International

Distributed to the book trade in Canada by Publishers Group West (PGW),
Toronto, Ontario

Contents

Children at Play

Foreword

For twenty-five years this book has inspired those who care about children. In an age when play is valued less and less, it stands out as a reminder of why play has always been part of childhood and why we must not stand by and allow it to die out.

During these years, the teachers in Waldorf kindergartens, where play is a central part of the education, have witnessed a steady decline in children's spontaneous ability to play. Modern children are accustomed to manufactured toys with defined purposes, television and films that present someone else's imagination, computers that use other people's programs, and classes in dance or sports in which someone instructs them in what to do. As a result, today's children can no longer bring forth their own strong, creative impulse to play. While a trained teacher can help children regain the world of play, it is a lengthy and difficult process. It would be so much better to keep the spirit of play alive in children in the first place and not let it be damaged, for it is a foundation for physical, social, and mental health.

Why is children's play declining? One reason is that in the United States and around the world, educators and parents have become increasingly preoccupied with early academics. There is a tremendous push for getting children to read at younger ages, and this spills over into other areas of learning as well. One public school kindergarten teacher told me that in her district the kindergarten curriculum was set by the legislature which demanded twenty minutes each of writing, reading, mathematics, science, social science, etc. each morning for children ages four-and-a-half to six. She then glanced over her shoulder, lowered her voice, and said to me, "You know, they don't allow any time for play, but I break the law every day and let my children play for fifteen minutes." Similar stories can be told all over the world.

The absence of open-ended play is also a problem for the school child, who used to create games with neighborhood friends, adjusting the rules as needed. Instead, from age five onward, many children join sports teams and are taught to play according to someone else's rules. They have little opportunity to exercise their own imagination or creative judgment. One parent who coached soccer for five-year-olds found it painful: "All they really want to do is get out on the field and play with the ball. Instead, they are supposed to be taught rules and skills. What are we doing to our children?" Another unfortunate result was seen by a college sports teacher. He loved baseball and bemoaned the fact that in high school and college, when young people were really ready to play the game, most had lost interest in it. As children they had participated in organized baseball with its stress and focus on winning; by adolescence they were burned out.

Why is play so important and what happens to children when it is eroded? Studies in Germany, Israel, and the United States show basically the same results regarding the importance of play: children who engage in creative play in early childhood tend to do better in all spheres of life as they grow older. They excel not only academically but also socially, emotionally, and physically. They tend to be more harmonious and less aggressive, and they show a better understanding of other people.

If children today are not playing as well as earlier children did, does this mean they are suffering in some way? According to research in the United States and Germany, there has been a serious deterioration in children's health over the past few decades. While the traditional childhood diseases have been nearly eradicated in developed countries, children instead show great increases in sleep and eating disorders, nervous ailments and stress, hyperactivity, and asthma and allergies. The overall decline in children's health in the United States is staggering. Government statistics show that in 1960 about 1.5 percent of children were considered disabled. By 1993 the number had grown to about 6.5 percent, and among poor children it was 10 percent. The conditions of modern life are endangering the health of our children, and their declining health goes hand in hand with their declining ability to play.

What do children need for a healthy life? One of the things is a relaxed, rhythmic lifestyle with plenty of time for creative play. They also need to see adults who enjoy their work and engage in it with active will, especially the basic human tasks of cooking, sewing, woodworking and the like. Children love to imitate adults at work, and this imitation is a cornerstone of play. Children also need simple, natural play materials out of which they can create their own toys, rather than finished toys that are defined and determine the play. Children need a chance to interact with the world of nature and with human beings, rather than with the technological world of televisions, videos, and computers. One can go on and on with such a list. In general, children thrive with a healthy, simple life, full of loving warmth, protected by secure boundaries and with opportunities to explore the world through play.

The children entering our kindergartens today are a wonderful group. They have a deep awareness of life and a great love of the earth and all that is on it. As one six-year-old recently said to me from the depths of his being, "I just love the earth, I just love it!" Such children need a healthy upbringing that includes plenty of opportunity for play, so that the love they feel now can ripen and become deeds of service later.

It is good to have this book back in print, for it is like a beacon of light to all who value play and want to include it in a child's life.

Joan Almon, Chair
Waldorf Kindergarten Association of North America

Preface

All the world's a stage,
And all the men and women merely players;
They have their exits and their entrances,
And one man in his time plays many parts . . .*

We may pursue Shakespeare's image and say that it is as children that these 'players' *rehearse* their parts — in their own forms of 'play', through the innumerable activities and games of childhood. There is nothing that human beings do, know, think, hope, and fear that has not been attempted, experienced, practised or at least anticipated in children's games.

In attempting to traverse this very wide field without losing our bearings, we shall, like the melancholy Jaques, have to take it bit by bit. Though as he does we begin with the infant 'mewling and puking in the nurse's arms', our progress will not necessarily be so strictly chronological as his, our emphasis being rather on the different qualities of play, which may extend through more than one phase of childhood. We shall remember, too, that behind the visible scene lies the invisible. The human being, though bound by laws of space and time and tied to the earth, stems from eternity and belongs to the cosmos; an animal by reason of his body, alive like tree and flower, committed to human

* Shakespeare, *As You Like It*, III. 7.

7

society, he remains, nevertheless, related in his inmost being to the all-embracing world of the spirit. That which is inmost and that which is all-embracing come so close together that it can be difficult to define the boundary between them. To adapt the words of Prospero: 'These our actors' are 'all spirits . . .'

Space and Time

Although the child occupies the surrounding space with his body, although with each heartbeat and breath he measures time, the nature of time and space is such that a great effort is needed on the part of the infant to perceive and investigate them. He experiences and becomes aware of the connection between time and space by means of innumerable early exercises and games. Is it near or far, attainable or unattainable? This makes the first attempts at grasping an object into an adventure. The rattle can be caught hold of, but not the brightly shining moon. The time between seeing the milk bottle in his mother's hands and tasting the first drops tests the child's patience to the utmost. Saint Paul says that through patience comes experience, but the little child is able to develop only an elementary kind of patience — a patience closely connected with trust — through a regular repetition of events.

The development of trust thus already starts with the infant; and we must already be at pains not to disturb this development by deceiving him. If we show him the milk bottle, then the meal should also follow. If we tell the child we are taking him for a walk, then it should be only when we are really taking him out and not just to make him look at his hat or begin to wave because we want to parade his intelligence to the relatives. Children are not clockwork machines. They can be turned into them for a time, and you can show off all their paces, but eventually you will have to pay dearly for it, if not always at the same time and in the same way.

By means of what he sees, grasps, moves, lets go again or drops, the child finds his relationship to space and time, to the laws of nature, to all those things which can later be measured, weighed and calculated. From the age of twelve months, one of my godsons devoted himself for many weeks to his own game with space and quantity. Whenever he had a large number of similar things at his disposal, such as balls, little bricks, plums or other fruit, or even six shining red plastic plates, he would distribute these objects around the room. He would look at the results for a while, and then head for each piece on his unsteady legs, laboriously pick it up and so gather all of them together again. He would look with satisfaction at what he had collected and then start to distribute them all over again. Still more pleasing than the rattle of the plates or the rolling of the plums was the way in which paper handkerchiefs floated silently to the ground. There they lay, silent and flat on the carpet until they were again heaped as a loose mass on the sofa. For weeks the mother wisely left the child at these games. In the same way she went for months with her son to the park where, day after day, he clambered up the same little slope to come clambering or rolling down it again. Depending on the weather, the child was covered in dust, or mud, or snow when he returned home — but always very happy and deeply satisfied. He had practised controlling his body and gaining command of his environment, and had enjoyed the pleasure of repetition.

Richard Harlacher[1] writes:

> For the child, toys are completely unpoetical experimental objects with which to penetrate the hallowed realms of physics. The exploration of physics, therefore, already starts long before secondary school. And the teacher of physics

would have a hard time if he had to start his teaching without the child's pre-school experiments.

Ball, rattle, spoon — all are dropped on to the floor. The sound is different each time. Through the continuous repetition, the ear learns to distinguish the different qualities of the sounds made by different objects. Many years later, when studying physics in school, he will stand leaning over a bridge testing how long something takes to hit the water — or the crew of a passing boat. He has meanwhile reached the stage of Galileo.

As soon as the young child's strength allows, plates and bowls become experimental objects: they sail through the air until a door or cupboard offers resistance and they fall to the ground robbed of all their strength. Experience of space is broadened in all directions from the purely vertical downward movement to the horizontal backward and forward and the vertical upward movements. As he becomes more expert in throwing, the child can begin to control and observe the trajectory of an object. A few years later it only remains to learn the proper name: parabola — and how to calculate it, of course. The shining spoon he throws serves as a kind of 'luminous marker' of the trajectory that helps to coordinate the target, the optic nerve and the force needed for the throw. The dimensions of space are conquered; distance is included in the child's increasing skill in judgment. Sound ranging comes next: the noise from the cupboard returns faster than that from the door. The effect of these efforts is ascertained and the experience used the next time . . .

If the balls and wooden blocks are of different colours, then the games also serve to develop the sense for colour. A ball flying through a patch of sunlight which lights it up for a moment enriches the child's experience of colour. A further development takes place when the child tries to pull the teddy-bear, which it has thrown out, back into its cot through the bars — at right angles to the bars! — at first complaining, then raging, and finally laughing through its tears, having finally grasped the principle of how to do it. We adults are wrong to find this 'funny'. What does the budding engineer think if we do not take his efforts seriously, or if we become impatient and 'help' him, because he manages to put the lid on the cardboard box correctly only at the tenth try?

But this is by no means all that children learn with their first toys. Hands, eyes, ears, nose and mouth all play a part in their discovery. Toys should really not all be made out of dead plastic material. How many people can still remember the different tastes of wood — unvarnished of course! Perhaps even a freshly cut piece from a willow branch? Leather tastes and smells different from rubber or, perhaps orris-root — out of fashion now as something for the first teeth to bite on. If you want to attach a bell to the pram, do not take the first one that comes to hand; rather try out a whole selection until you find one with a pleasing sound. We should not be indifferent to the materials that surround the child, for the very reason that it does not understand them, and because all impressions are assimilated indiscriminately and at random.

Modern psychological and medical research continually comes across the decisive influence that the impressions and experiences of earliest childhood have on the physical and spiritual development of the human being. The catalogue of parental mistakes that create 'complexes and frustrations' in the infant is of such magnitude — and varies so much from one author to another — that often the mere study of them can create 'complexes and frustrations' in the poor parents. Since every mistake has its corresponding opposite, it is no wonder that confusion and insecurity become widespread in nurseries and the minds of parents. One example: the infant needs attention, care and stimulation. If these are missing it falls ill and ends up in hospital. This we have learnt. My sister made me aware of the opposite fault and its consequences in dealing with children. She has worked for many years as a children's nurse in families, hospitals and homes and has found that the early experimental games of children are often interrupted unnecessarily. A young mother sits by the cot of her first child (for the second there is already less time!) and watches how it tries over and over again to place a red cube on a blue one on its point. After a while she has watched this long enough and asks: 'And where is your lovely dolly?' The child abandons its bricks, looks for the doll and begins to lick its face — licks and licks until the mother brings Teddy on the scene: 'Grrr, grrr, here comes dear old teddy!' The child turns away from the doll and takes hold of Teddy. It twists him around in its hands and finally moves one leg up and down, up and down, until — well, until the mother becomes bored and draws the child's attention to its ball. Politely it lets itself be distracted a third time and plays with the ball. In this way the mother spends an enjoyable afternoon and is entirely unaware how she *disrupts* her child's perseverance and ability to concentrate. She prevents it getting used to persevering at an activity, and thoroughly occupying itself with something over any length of time.

She will then later complain that the four-year-old will not stay at any game. He will be continually hanging on to her apron strings: 'What shall I do now, Mummy?' Still later comes trouble with homework, which will take the whole evening because he cannot concentrate longer than a minute on his work before having to look at something else. Finally the school psychologist is asked for an effective and speedy solution to the problem. If he does not have one, then he is just no use. Yet it was the mother herself who spoilt the child's perseverance and staying power — whether with the best of intentions, or without even thinking about it.

When modern educational psychologists and those defending the teaching of children to read as early as possible record that a child does not remain longer than seventy-five, at most ninety, seconds at one and the same activity, they can only have made their observations on children already disturbed in their ability to concentrate.

There are infants whose staying-power can be absolutely counted on. I remember two like that; neither of them had reached the age of two when the following incidents happened.

One was visiting his aunt in whose garden there was a very high swing. Before lunch the small guest, who had already had his meal, was placed on the swing and given a good push. After lunch, someone went down and lifted him from the now only gently moving swing, on which he had spent the interval with great pleasure. The other one was placed by his mother on a stool which stood on a chair at the table. He threw two pins into a glass bottle, shook them about, and then emptied them on to the table. Thereupon, he stuck the pins carefully into a pin-cushion, enjoyed the result, and then pulled them out again and dropped them tinkling into the jar. He continued doing this until his mother came back from the dairy. She had no need to fear that the child would become bored with his activity before her return. However, this mother could not have relied so firmly on the perseverance of any of her other children at a game.

Now, one need not think that such great persistence is just a sign of natural indolence, not to say downright laziness. The boy on the swing has grown into a specially hard-working man, and the child with the bottle has also grown up to be lively and useful at many things.

After coming to grips with surrounding objects, the next step in conquering space is to start moving oneself. Crawling is the first temporary solution. Some children jump this stage, others perfect it to an astonishing degree. 'Mummy, if my little sister gets ill, she will have to crawl to hospital, won't she?' reflected a brother of nearly three.

Hardly has the child learnt to crawl before it tries to gain height. A delightful means of discovering differences in height is a flight of stairs, a wooden flight in a living room being the most comfortable, of course. Crawling up can be learnt quickly. This can also be done more ceremoniously as, for example, by putting a favourite building brick on to the next step before climbing after it. It is much more difficult to come down. It is quite a relief for the mother when she knows that the child turns reliably each time and does not try to make a descent head first! Only then have the stairs been conquered, and for many years they remain a favourite spot for playing. A. A. Milne expresses this particular delight of childhood in his poem *Halfway Down*:

Halfway down the stairs
Is a stair
Where I sit.
There isn't any
Other stair
Quite like
It.
I'm not at the bottom,
I'm not at the top;
So this is the stair
Where
I always
Stop.

It is not only that a step is the ideal height for a sitting child, but that the adult, too, sitting on the stairs, has suddenly become accessible in a wonderful way. The child can sit down so that it is just as tall as the adult or even taller. Lap, shoulders, hair — no one needs to lift the child. With a few steps it can reach where it wants to go.

But then, amidst great rejoicing, the first steps are taken

15

— upright on two legs. Space, which has grown familiar through play, is conquered step by step. It is an effort to take one step after another — all one's life. The small child will often still hold out its hand: 'Help me!' or even both arms: 'Carry me!' And for weeks after learning to walk, a child will always trot about with its arms raised, without, however, expecting or wishing adult help. What is it that helps it along, until it is secure on its feet?

Children love to be swung forward by the arms between two adults. All his life, man tries to save steps and surmount obstacles by the easiest means. There are the scooters and tricycles, the first real bicycle, sledges and skis, roller- and ice-skates. Later comes the elation of having a moped puttering away beneath you with the wind blowing in your face. And so it continues, from the car to the rocket.

But before man learned to drive or even ride, he had to explore his environment, step by step. This also applies to the child. The experience of seeing a distant goal gradually come closer, of being able to take only one step at a time, is part of human life! Somebody on foot experiences something different from somebody who sees the world only from his car, and he gets to know that absolutely basic measurement — the human pace. As an introduction to his geometry lessons, my father used to tell his class to sketch an outline of the school buildings and grounds to the scale of four millimetres to two paces. All the drawings were different — the smaller the steps the bigger the drawing — but in themselves they were all to scale. This way of experiencing one's 'own scale' in relation to the general measurement of the metre, derived from the world's circumference, had a strong effect on the children.

In trying to cover distance faster and with less effort, it may well be that we find something at the other end which is more important than the experiences of the journey. But what is really gained if time is just 'whiled away' or even 'killed'? Time, of which each of us possesses only a limited amount, cannot be bought or rented. There is a strange law in connection with it, which is again related to the 'human scale'. If time is filled, it passes very quickly, though it remains a long time and in great detail in the memory, and provides material for innumerable stories. Time which is empty, on the other hand, passes very slowly and is hardly remembered at all. We speak of boredom when time is empty like that. I must still have been very small when my grandmother started giving me tips and advice on how to fill empty time — periods of waiting and the like — by recalling important memories for which otherwise there is not much time, or poems learnt by heart. I am sure these conversations with my grandmother have contributed to the fact that boredom has always remained something unknown to me.

'Whiling away time' is just as sinister and suspect an expression as 'killing' it. Who could have an interest in making people 'while away' their allotted time? Who is it that tries to prevent man's thinking, feeling and willing being strengthened and co-ordinated and encourages their dissipation?

The Cosmos

Already at a very early age, the child enjoys the game of hide-and-seek. The infant's games of bo-peep or peek-a-boo with mother or little brother or sister round the side of the pram undergo a change with the toddler who keeps his eyes shut and imagines he is no longer there. One child of eighteen months used to turn round and then ask pensively: 'Where is Mummy now?'

These games reflect the transition from there to here, from the spiritual to the physical world, which takes place every morning on waking up. A little boy who could already say a few words at the age of nine months had great difficulties in waking up each morning. For some time he would moan and whimper to himself until he sat up and said firmly: 'There!'. Then he really *was* there — awake and happy. Infants' games of hide-and-seek are games of sleeping and waking or day and night.

'Where is Mummy now?' reflects mankind's age-old question: 'Where is the sun during the night?' All the singing games and round-dances of children originate in the ancient cult-dances which expressed man's relationship to the planets and the stars. This seems to be expressed quite clearly in the following rhyme:

> Sally go round the sun,
> Sally go round the moon,
> Sally go round the chimney pots
> On a Sunday afternoon!

Even modern sport has its origin in the stars, although one would hardly any longer think so. In ancient Greek times, the symbols of the zodiac were fixed around the stadium at Olympia. The athletes followed the orbit of the sun. Many of the rhythms that can be observed on earth go back to cosmic rhythms — even if they are not all as obvious as the seasons or the tides.

On the effect of rhythm on children Rudolf Steiner writes[2]:

> For early childhood it is important to realize the value of children's songs, for example, as a means of education. They must make a pretty and rhythmical impression on the senses; the beauty of the sound is to be valued more than the meaning. The more living the impression made on eye and ear, the better. Dancing movements in a musical rhythm have a powerful influence in building up the physical organs, and this too should not be undervalued.

The heartbeat of the mother is the lullaby of the unborn child. Once it was discovered that the new-born infant also finds this rhythm soothing, people ingeniously hit on the idea of playing a tape recording of the mother's heartbeat to soothe him. For a time the child falls for this trick until eventually he notices that no one is there. One is reminded of the fairy tale of Hansel and Gretel: the children sit alone in the forest and think they can hear the knocking of their father's axe; in fact it is only the wind knocking a dry branch against a tree. They finally realize that they have been deserted. If, however, the child is put in a cradle, then this new rhythm also soothes him and proves to him that someone is there, rocking him.

Very soon the baby in the cradle becomes a 'rider' on its parents' knees and experiences the rhythm of its first nursery rhymes:

Ride a cock-horse to Banbury Cross
To see a fine lady ride a white horse;
With rings on her fingers and bells on her toes,
She shall have music wherever she goes.

Or the child learns to clap hands to the rhythm of
Pat a cake, pat a cake,
Baker's man . . .
Years before it reaches the age for fairy tales, the child's imagination has also thus been stimulated and its vocabulary extended beyond the ordinary daily usage. The bouncing ball is a source of rhythm. The ball, a perfect sphere, is a likeness of the earth, the sun, all the planetary bodies. An indispensable toy: from the giant ball, majestically rolling across the lawn, to the excitedly bouncing little rubber balls; from the soft, cloth ball of the infant to the catch-ball that father throws almost to the sky, and the football that can be kicked so hard — each conveys a small part of the great game of the heavenly bodies.

Who can still juggle with three or even four balls? Who manages to pass the 'test' against the wall, with all its strict rules? A playground should have a wall for ball games, so that this exciting art does not die out. Ball games are certainly impoverished if kicking starts too soon and experience of the bouncing and flying ball goes short. The ball on a string is like a moon in orbit, held by gravity and, incidentally, like our moon, always with the same side facing the centre.

The balloon is an extraordinary ball — its inevitable ascent into the heavens leaves children either with a feeling of ecstatic delight or heartbreaking sorrow, depending on their temperament. Soap bubbles are also balls of a very special nature. The little dream worlds float up and away around the child, filled and carried by his own breath; he sees them gleaming and changing in a magical display of colours — until they become little black spots and burst. But the creative breath can go on making new ones. A painting by Fritz Burger in the Kurpfälzische Museum in Heidelberg is called *Creations*. Among these 'creations' there are spherical forms, in every way similar to soap-bubbles. And Christian Morgenstern in *Palmström* describes how 'Korf hears of a distant cousin, a sorceress, who blows planets from a lather of herbs . . .'.

All spinning-tops — from the big humming ones, to the tiny ones like clock wheels — make cosmic movements visible. It is very sad that there is no room left on our streets for the good old whipping-top! The rolling hoop, too, like all wheels, is basically the image of a solar system circling through space. A pity that this enjoyable game is also just too dangerous to play on our pavements! Perhaps skipping with a rope can still be counted among the games connected with the oscillating and circling of the cosmos.

Only someone who has owned a tall swing during his childhood can appreciate the happiness a swing can give. Ours was about fifteen feet high, and the experience of becoming alternately light and heavy, quite apart from the physical excercise, was unforgettable. When you swing on a really tall swing, there is even a moment when you can experience the phenomenon of weightlessness so much talked about these days. The swing — like the hammock — is also a cradle 'extended beyond the infant's first years'. Like the cradle, it brings harmony and calm into a soul which has been disturbed. 'The hammock is used by whoever needs it,' a mother of many children said.

You can even play with the sun — with the long shadows, with the short shadows it makes; you can chase shadows; you can use a mirror to reflect the light, or a prism to create the colours of the rainbow, or even burn holes in school books with a lens. Again and again children will try to feel what the blue or red sunlight from a coloured window feels like. A bit of coloured glass to look through can be a magic window for a child.

The sun can be experienced by every child. With the

moon and stars it is already more difficult, since it never becomes properly night in our brightly-lit cities. At least, therefore, we should try in the holidays to let our children experience a moonless starry sky and show them the different constellations and planets. The appearance of the moon, too, should be familiar to them in its different phases before they get to seeing close-ups of it on television. An eclipse of the moon, a beautiful, full moon in all its solemnity on a winter night, should be enough reason to fetch a child out of bed for once in the middle of the night; even if the experience does sink into the subconscious, still the child has had it, and it helps him to become familiar with the cosmos. Hans Carossa writes[3]:

> Once my mother woke me up during the night and carried me down into the street. People stood there together, murmured amongst themselves and observed the sky. A hand turned my head in the direction everybody was looking and a voice said: 'Can you see the comet?' It appeared in such a shimmer of light that I could not overlook it. A long arch of white light stood in the blackness of the night above the village. The patient waiting and staring of the people, their almost frightened whispers, the lonely distance of the resplendent arch, all this was indelibly inscribed on my memory; however, it affected me much more strongly later on, recalling it, than on the actual night. Hardly three years old, I was not ready for strong feelings of fear or awe; I sat on my mother's arm and felt through her sure running of the world.

The many beautiful songs of sun, moon and stars should accompany every childhood. That a rainbow should be duly admired and celebrated need hardly be mentioned. But one had better think carefully what to answer afterwards when the child inevitably asks: 'Where is the rainbow now?' An optical explanation is not a suitable answer for small children.

The Four Elements

'They enjoyed playing in the elements today!' said two mothers happily to one another at the close of a long Sunday. On the rocky bank of the stream a campfire had been burning and the four boys played between fire, stream and rock.

In playing with the four elements — earth, water, air and fire — the child takes up for the first time the most ancient task of mankind, pronounced in the words of the Creator that he should 'have dominion . . . over all the earth.'

The child often first meets the element of earth in the form of sand. How splendid are the sand-pies and the tunnelled sandcastles, which later develop into fortresses, runs for marbles, gardens and settlements. Its wonders never fail: dry sand trickles through the hand, damp sand stands firm, really wet sand pours. Unfortunately it is not found everywhere in great quantities, and thus the joy of the child is doubled on experiencing a real beach. Some children take sand-baths like chickens. I once had a three-year-old guest who used to take dust-baths in the black ash from the boiler which was used to spread on a nearby path. — Well, not everybody is able to have sand. Some have clay instead, but not for castles or tunnels; the pies become rolls and loaves of bread which dry to the hardness of stone in the sun. In the end, playing with mud and clay leads to modelling. Actual stones test the child's growing strength, and harbour different dangers according to size.

However, the first element with which the child plays is

water. An especially early reminiscence of playing with water is described by Stefan Andres in his autobiographical book[4]. As he grew up in a mill, he had many opportunities for playing with water:

I loved the water behind the low sandstone wall. Without completely giving myself up to it, that is climbing in, I could completely immerse my hands and arms in it. I stood leaning over the soft stone of the wall, my sleeves rolled up as high as possible, and twirled my arms in all that water . . .

The game simply consisted in stirring my arms in the water. I tried to grab it with both hands and hold it, but it would slop away. I could feel its heaviness, but only for a second, then all that remained in my hands were a few drops. And the game started all over again. The feeling of holding the smooth body of water in one's arms, till they grew painfully cold and stiff and red, was very pleasant to me. And the light on the water, the sky which broke into pieces, and suddenly part of a face which swayed about and flowed away . . . there were moments of fright, of delight, and then the state of purely sensuous pleasure returned again: the water was smooth and cool, flowing so beautifully and holding me tight, until I felt a smack on my behind and a hand took me by the scruff of the neck and carried me home. The water had gradually taken hold of my whole small person and it was surprising that I did not continually have a cold.

Such primal experiences still occasionally enter games with water when the child is already older — games with watering-cans, rubber animals, ships of all sorts — made of bark, paper, wood, plastic and of nutshells containing small candles. The latter serve as 'fire-boats' between the paper-boats in sea-battles, which can be waged in any trough of water. If the weather prevents this outdoors, the ships can be placed on imaginary water. I know children who used to say: 'Mummy, give us the Thames!' Mother would spread out a roll of blue crêpe paper on the floor and then the boats were fetched and new ones folded, and the game was soon in progress.

When flat pebbles are skimmed across the water so that they bounce on its surface — so many times! — then laws of nature enter into the very flesh and blood, and later in physics it is only necessary to understand what has been grasped long before. The same applies when one entrusts one's own body to the watery element, whether in swimming or wading in fast flowing water, or floating on a raft, an air-mattress, or in a boat.

Frozen water, too, is enticing for games. A thin layer of snow is enough to permit a 'slide' across the school playground — if the headmaster also permits it! More snow allows snowballing and sledging. The wetter kind of snow can be rolled into a snowman or used to build an igloo. If it is well built and thoroughly frozen through, such an igloo can sometimes still be left standing in the middle of a green meadow when warmer weather comes — although its walls may be rather thin. Where enough snow falls, allowing one to put on one's skis at the front door — well, some people are lucky! In other places there are large areas of ice which can be used for all sorts of things.

Mud and marshy ground constitute the transition between water and earth and are especially attractive to children. Fortunately these days there are rubber boots and easy-care clothes, as well as the washing machine, so that we need not make a fuss as if something unheard of has happened when, once again, muddy little apparitions arrive on the door step. My neighbour and I still have to laugh today when we remember the autumn day when four of our children slid continuously over a muddy board into the clayey water of a building site excavation. We finally caught the four little 'piglets' — not without some difficulty — scrubbed them from top to toe, put them to bed, and not one of them caught a cold.

The following story about a game with the element of air

Building an Igloo

Use rolls of snow, as if for a snowman; or make the building blocks like and-pies in a small plastic bucket or a waxed conical wooden mould.

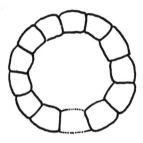

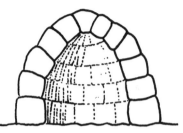

The ground-plan is circular and the inner diameter about one metre (three feet). The bigger it becomes the more difficult it is to build!

2 In elevation our igloo is higher than that of the Eskimos. Only cut out the entrance when it becomes difficult to manage from the outside.

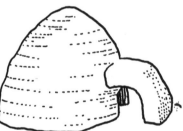

3 Here the key-stone is fitted into place.

4 Finally the igloo is smoothed over on the outside and an entrance tunnel built on. It is even possible to put in a small ice window.

appeared many years ago in Reader's Digest in Frances Fowler's *The Day We Flew the Kites*[5].

'String!' shouted Brother, bursting into the kitchen. 'We need lots more string.'

It was Saturday. As always, it was a busy one, for 'Six days shalt thou labor and do all thy work' was taken seriously then. Outside, Father and Mr. Patrick next door were doing chores. Inside the two houses, Mother and Mrs. Patrick were engaged in spring cleaning. Such a windy March day was ideal for 'turning out' clothes closets. Already woollens flapped on back-yard clothes lines.

Somehow the boys had slipped away to the back lot with their kites. Now, even at the risk of having Brother impounded to beat carpets, they had sent him for more string. Apparently there was no limit to the heights to which kites would soar today.

My mother looked out of the window. The sky was piercing blue; the breeze fresh and exciting. Up in all that blueness sailed great puffy billows of clouds. It had been a long hard winter, but today was Spring.

Mother looked at the sitting room, its furniture disordered for a Spartan sweeping. Again her eyes wavered toward the window. 'Come on, girls! Let's take string to the boys and watch them fly the kites a minute.'

On the way we met Mrs. Patrick, laughing guiltily, escorted by her girls.

There never was such a day for flying kites! God doesn't make two such days in a century. We played all our fresh line into the boys' kites and still they soared. We could hardly distinguish the tiny, orange-coloured specks. Now and then we slowly reeled one in, finally bringing it dipping and tugging to earth, for the sheer joy of sending it up again. What a thrill to run with them, to the right, to the left, and see our poor, earth-bound movements reflected minutes later in the majestic sky-dance of the kites! We wrote wishes on slips of paper and slipped them over the string. Slowly, irresistibly, they climbed up until they reached the kites. Surely all such wishes would be granted!

Even our fathers dropped hoe and hammer and joined us.

Our mothers took their turn laughing like schoolgirls. Their hair blew out of their pompadours and curled loose about their cheeks; their gingham aprons whipped about their legs. Mingled with our fun was something akin to awe. The grown-ups were really playing with us! Once I looked at Mother and thought she looked actually pretty. And her over forty!

We never knew where the hours went on that hill-top day. There were no hours, just a golden, breezy Now. I think we were all a little beyond ourselves. Parents forgot their duty and their dignity; children forgot their combativeness and small spites. 'Perhaps it's like this in the Kingdom of Heaven,' I thought confusedly.

It was growing dark before, drunk with sun and air, we all stumbled sleepily back to the houses. I suppose we had some sort of supper. I suppose there must have been a surface tidying up, for the house on Sunday looked decorous enough.

The strange thing was we didn't mention that day afterwards, I felt a little embarrassed. Surely none of the others had thrilled to it as deeply as I. I locked the memory up in that deepest part of me where we keep 'the things that cannot be and yet are.'

The years went on, then one day I was scurrying about my own kitchen in a city apartment, trying to get some work out of the way while my three-year-old insistently cried her desire to 'go park and see ducks.'

'I *can't* go!' I said. 'I have this and this to do, and when I'm through I'll be too tired to walk that far.'

My mother, who was visiting us, looked up from the peas she was shelling. 'It's a wonderful day,' she offered 'really warm, yet there's a fine fresh breeze. It reminds me of that day we flew the kites.'

I stopped in my dash between stove and sink. The locked door flew open, and with it a gush of memories. I pulled off my apron. 'Come on,' I told my little girl. 'You're right, it's too good a day to miss.'

Another decade passed. We were in the aftermath of a great war. All evening we had been asking our returned soldier, the youngest Patrick boy, about his experiences as a prisoner of

war. He had told freely, but now for a long time he had been
silent. What was he thinking of — what dark and dreadful
things?

'Say!' A smile twitched on his lips. 'Do you remember . . .
no, of course you wouldn't. It probably didn't make the
impression on you it did on me'.

I hardly dared speak. 'Remember what?'

'I used to think of that day a lot in PW camp, when things
weren't too good. Do you remember the day we flew the
kites?' Winter came, and the sad duty of a call of condolence on
Mrs. Patrick, recently widowed. I dreaded the call. I couldn't
imagine how Mrs. Patrick would face life alone.

We talked a little of my family and her grandchildren and the
changes in the town. Then she was silent, looking down at her
lap. I cleared my throat. Now I must say something about her
loss, and she would begin to cry.

When she looked up, Mrs. Patrick was smiling. 'I was just
sitting here thinking,' she said. 'Henry had such fun that day.
Frances, do you remember the day we flew the kites?'

Quite apart from that splendid description of a game with
the element of air, this wonderful story shows how a
seemingly senseless game, for which the spring-cleaning
was sacrificed, could be a source of help many years later in
life.

When it comes to learning to know the element of air
through play, town children are again at a disadvantage. It
is just for these children that one has to create the
opportunity to measure their own strength against the force
of the wind. On windy days one should take them out
where it does not matter if they are blown around in their
rain-coats like leaves. Little flags and windmills make it all
the more fun.

At home parachutes made of tissue paper — nicest are real
Japanese paper napkins — can be released from the balcony
or window. The seedpods of sycamore or spruce trees,
which spin like little propellers when dropped, can be

brought back from an outing or from the local park. All kinds of gliders can be made, or the ever popular 'swallow' folded out of a sheet of paper. Which one of my sons was it, who told me how they fixed harmless little crackers to these swallows and sent them gliding into enemy classrooms? Who knows the 'Montgolfier', the hot air balloon? Shaped like a pear and made of tissue paper, and heated with a wad of cotton-wool soaked in methylated spirits, it floats off ceremoniously and silently. This can be the crowning event of a children's party. It is also the rising hot air that moves the 'stove-snake'. This mysterious creation, cut in spiral form from an exercise book cover and fixed to the end of a knitting needle which is then stuck in half a potato, constantly revolves in a spiral on the stove or radiator, in the same way as the angels at Christmas are turned by the warmth of four candles.

Real flames are rarely seen by town children. Even the Christmas tree does not have real candles, but electric substitutes. And yet how lovely flames are! Stefan Andres writes[4]:

> In one of the outhouses, my father stood in front of the baking oven and pushed in the fragrant pieces of beech wood. I stood beside him and watched the flames playing. Little riders sprang here and there on the wood, gesticulated with their hands, leapt, stretched themselves upwards for a second and danced. The flames no longer wanted to dance alone; one jumped into another, made the second one bigger and thus grew bigger and brighter itself. After that no flame was alone longer than a moment. They were continually transformed, leapt out at the stone, and at the same time sang a soft, hissing song. The pieces of wood, however, lay motionless for a long time, just as Father had placed them. Finally they blackened at the top edge where the flames were dancing. And then they suddenly broke in two with a slight crack. This made all kinds of wild figures and terrible, distorted faces appear, beings which had surely been shut up in the wood and which the fire had lured out. At

last the flames became tired and went away. But where did they go to? I asked my father that, who was also staring into the open baking oven. 'The flames?' — 'Yes, a moment ago they were still here!'

'Where do they go? They go out, so one says!' Father shook his head. 'You might just as well ask where the wood is. That isn't there any more either!'

Nevertheless, it is not the country where games with fire play an important role, even less the centres of towns. Fire games thrive on the edge of towns — on waste-land, amongst the rubble, the waste-tips of coal pits and rubbish dumps. In these places small fires flare up again and again. Perhaps holes are knocked in old tin cans, dried wood-shavings put inside and the tins swung round on long wires. A dozen boys march along in the fading evening light across a waste dump, one behind the other. Each one carries a burning piece of conveyor-belt as a torch — a wild counterpart to the lantern processions that become increasingly popular as a way of ending children's parties in the autumn. One specially gifted kite designer I know let a kite rise at night with a round yellow lantern attached — an impressive spectacle.

From my own childhood I remember a Christmas Eve when I was about three-and-a-half years old and I was playing with my little sister in our nursery. Both of us had already been bathed and were wearing our Sunday best. Then I discovered a drawer which I had not known existed until then, filled with the finest soft grey sand. The waste of leaving such a treasure unused struck me with great force — and with eager little hands we strewed the marvellous stuff around the room. Later, after the distribution of the presents, I had to watch how my poor, tired-out mother had to clean our room again. After that I knew what ash was. We had got at the ash-box!

In the age of central heating, this kind of thing cannot

happen any more, but occasionally a little boy comes to me on a visit, who, before he started going to school, would solemnly say 'good morning' to the fire in my stove during the winter. At home he rarely sees a flame since it is all electrically heated and his father does not even smoke.

How marvellous it is to make an excursion in winter through crunching snow, and then lay a lattice of dry twigs on it — have a red blazing fire, a pot of tea simmering away, apples fried on the end of a stick — such an experience fathers can still give their children even in this day and age.

Some children have a passion for fire; they always have matches on them, and try to ignite something absolutely *everywhere* — in the garden, in the school grounds, in their room — and one lives in constant fear of fire. Keeping them under observation is sometimes simply not possible, prohibition and punishment without effect.

When a fire is built often enough *with* adults, the prohibition of lighting fires without an adult becomes easier to enforce. Then, too, the danger of fire and how to handle it is understood much sooner. Those in particular who try to educate their children with a minimum of rules and prohibitions should impress this *fundamental* rule on them:

There is nothing bad, terrible or humiliating that can happen to a child that would not become worse, more terrible or more humiliating, if it were concealed from his parents.

As to its use in connection with fire, I used to tell the story of a friend whose eight-year-old son came running to his father one Sunday afternoon. He had made a fire with some friends at the little shed behind the barn on the farm where they were living, and now the shed was ablaze! The father was able to call the farmer. With the aid of a few passers-by a chain was formed and the blaze extinguished with buckets of water before it had a chance to set fire to the barn, which was filled with the year's harvest. Only then did the parents miss their son. Late at night the little fire-bug came creeping home, filled with fear and remorse, and was *praised* by his father! Such a story, told over and over, is more effective than many admonitions.

There is something else to be remembered nowadays; however practical and easy it may be to look after children's clothing made of such materials as nylon, dralon, helanca, in a fire they are extremely dangerous. Burning cotton flies away in the form of light ash, wool does not easily ignite and goes out quickly, but burning artificial fibres eat their way deep into the flesh as a viscous, seething pulp.

Nevertheless, to light a fire, keep it under control, and carefully extinguish it again are experiences to which all children have a right; one should not deny it them. They need these experiences for their harmonious development.

As there is the biogenetic basic law according to which every living creature, man or animal (right from the single-celled organism), lives through a short recapitulation of the development of its species in its embryonic development, so there is also the 'psychogenetic law' that in the spiritual realm something comparable happens: every child in the course of its development repeats primitive stages of civilization, or at least indications of them.

Messing about in water, making paper swallows, and experimenting with the campfire ensure a sound and healthy approach to modern technology — one worthy of human beings. Giving children perfected technical toys too early paralyses their technical inventiveness, which alone brings progress. Who needs an electric railway if he cannot knock a nail in or saw a piece off a plank of wood? He may soon learn how to operate a railway, but never develop new ideas, never learn how to do an improvised repair until the ready-made spare part arrives.

An eight-year-old boy who had lots of technical toys,

was one day visiting a strange farm, and the gate — about four feet high — was closed to keep a two-year-old off the road. When his parents came to collect him, the eight-year-old broke into tears: He had been locked in! — The thought of climbing over the gate had not occurred to him.

Another boy straight away destroyed all technical toys and played instead with dolls and little animals, and used nails, a hammer and saw. When he was nine years old, his parents discovered that their son had relaid the electric wiring in his grandfather's cellar — faultlessly. Thereupon they gave him a voltameter and since that time, whenever the now grown-up boy goes to visit friends' houses, things which need to be repaired are laid out ready for him.

Plants and Animals

When we say: Children's paradise — what kind of a picture do we conjure up? A garden with a large stretch of grass, a tree for climbing, singing birds and flowers — some large as faces and others small enough for dwarfs to look at? A beach with sand and seashells, seaweed and crabs, jellyfish and starfish? A farm with all kinds of animals, with kittens and chickens? The edge of a pond with rushes and frogs? It is characteristic of a paradise that man is not the only living being in it — and thus animals or plants, or both, belong to a true children's paradise.

The things a child experiences and does in its paradise range from dream-like immersion in the moods of nature to eager activity or far-reaching imaginative games. The first is described by Hans Carossa[3]:

> There were hours when all I wanted to do was to roam around in the fields among the cattle with their ringing bells, to look in their eyes, to feel their mighty, reassuring breath, to press myself against their heavy warm bodies, despite the danger from their horns and hooves. Yet their animal presence induced in me a state of inexplicably sorrowful anticipation which I never experienced among people. I looked to see whether I could discover something similar in other children, but since I could not, I thought I was alone in the world with my feelings. If at these times Father or Mother, lessons or prayers entered my thoughts, I rejected such memories as unbearably alien, as if, under the spell of the animal world, my only desire was to be animal and I had no wish to be released from the innocent dullness of animal life, until I would finally jump in a kind of fright and run home, very glad to emerge again into the normal human world.

Karl Foerster, the father of the modern shrub garden, writes[6]:

The sight of three brothers occupying themselves in a garden, each in his own way, already offers a picture of three different future developments. My one brother, the shipbuilder and technician, always liked to sow things in his garden which would burst forth from the soil with great show and effect, or he would play with ships in the water trough. When the earth started to crack above the seeds, he would already be inquisitively poking at it. My other brother, who became a thinker, made himself a den for reading in the elder tree. I – six years old – would carry watering cans past it to my flower garden, in which I was especially interested in having clear and striking colour effects; one brother impressed another by his little garden plans as, for example, by a mighty bed of mignonette: appreciation of the scent of these plain flowers promoted the designer of the flower-bed into the adult class.

Our sister and the cluster of sword-lilies in her garden became inseparable in our imagination; one magnificent bloom of hers was broken off and found lying somewhere, still fresh. In the midst of her indignation about it, Mother quickly painted a picture of the flower for her – this transformed the situation. In any other sphere than gardening, our mother's indescribably cheerful, ever-present sharing of our joy in the activity and in our individually named and cared for sheds and tools, would not have been so apparent.

After half a lifetime, a breath of the heavenly delight of our early gardening life with Mother still blows through our life.

The American journalist and thinker, Lincoln Steffens, writes in his autobiography[7]:

My father, mother, and others always wondered why I spent so much time over on the American River bottom: a washed-out place, where no one else ever went. Why not ride in the streets or the good country roads? I could not explain very well. The river bottom was all gravel and sand, cut up by the seasonal floods and left raw and bare of all but dead, muddied brush and trees. I remember how it disappointed me the first time I saw it, the day I rode over there on my new pony. Since then I had filled it up with Indians, Turks, beavers, and wild beasts and made it a beautiful scene of romance and adventure. But I could not tell everybody that!

Sometimes a children's paradise may strike adults as strange. I myself have seen with what untroubled happiness two little children and two young cats played together throughout a lovely, long summer afternoon with dead mice that the mother cat untiringly supplied.

In a country, or less 'thoroughly civilized' environment, intimate encounters between children and animals and plants occur practically without our help and in all different forms. Festive enhancement and highlighting of such experiences can be made possible with very little effort. For the town child, however, the opportunity for such encounters must be created with careful consideration, so that he does not remain a stranger to nature for the whole of his life. Holidays in the country, walks with well-chosen resting places can already make up for much.

But certain experiences every child should have for himself: certain areas of life have to be experienced and assimilated in depth as a child, so that later, in different places and under unaccustomed conditions, one notices the teeming life which would otherwise be missed.

Children should not dig only in sterile sand; digging in the living earth leads to encounters with worms, insects, centipedes and the wonderful little glowing-red spiders. If one turns the flat stones in shallow water one finds all kinds of swimming, crawling and clinging things that live there. A man told me how, as a boy, together with his sister, he set about killing and eradicating all the eelpouts — the fat-headed little fish of the area — to free nature's beauty of all such 'miscreations'. Today, our one-time 'beautifier of nature' works full-time in nature conservancy.

Tall grass intermingled with flowers, with innumerable

creatures humming about it and crawling through it —
larks high in the sky, frogs, slow-worms or snails on the
ground — a lawn is no substitute for this. A wood in spring
with its fresh new foliage, ringing with the chirping of
birds, with flowers and blooming bushes, and lazy,
blue-shimmering dung-beetles on the ground, indeed a
wood at any time of year — with all its manifold gifts of
berries, mushrooms, fir-cones, acorns and beech-nuts —
belongs of right to the necessary experiences of childhood.
Cultivated land, in its changes from ploughing to sowing or
planting and reaping — the child has to see where the
cleanly packaged foodstuffs in the supermarket originate!
For this reason, too, a visit to the cow-shed is indispensable.
Meeting a little calf is a special treat.

What else? Climbing trees — feeding chickens —
watching a bird hatching and rearing its young — playing
with kittens — picking flowers — gathering fruit — sowing
seeds and watching them sprout.

Every child should at least have held an animal. Some
children indefatigably bring creatures home: kittens,
beetles, young birds, tadpoles and newts. Then it is up to
the parents to decide how much they can cope with and
what the animal means to the child.

For a number of reasons, many people today are unable
or unwilling to keep either a dog or a cat and when one
cannot decide either for the long-lived bird, or the
short-lived hamster, one should once, perhaps, provide the
children with the unforgettable experience of an insect
metamorphosis. To gather big, hairy catepillars off sting-
ing-nettles in the spring is a very good tip. Food can be
found even in towns in some neglected corner; and whether
it is the peacock-butterfly or the painted-lady that finally
hatches out of the chrysalis, the delight of the children is
equally great. Or one can put a few of the ugly grey larvae

of the dragon-fly into an open aquarium with plants in it. They eat flies, little worms and small pieces of meat, and can also go hungry for some time. Then, one day in early summer, the empty chrysalis hangs on a plant stalk, and at the window there sits the magnificent, newly emerged dragon-fly.

It is funny to observe the names children give to things they have not seen before, and for which they do not know the name. Out of the dark earth of the garden climbed a goldsmith-beetle, a shiny and shimmering gold-green, with red legs. The small sons of the mining-official well knew what a miner does under the earth, but this marvel — 'Mother, *a mine-foreman!*' After that, this grand name remained in the family for the agile beetle.

A child's passionate wish to keep or own an animal can lead to understanding care for them, or to all kinds of misadventures. One teacher's son tried again and again to hatch birds' eggs in bed. Of course they always broke! During the summer a boy in the second class at school occasionally brought home tins with tadpoles or small fish. Three times on his expeditions he left a pair of new shoes standing by the pond — a high price to pay for the creepy-crawlies. Every available creature — size permitting — is at some time or another transported in a boy's pocket. Be it frogs, newts, kittens, mice, birds, lizards or caterpillars, accidents cannot always be avoided. And if they manage to survive the transport, not a few animals are loved to death. Others perish because the little animal lover stands the cage in the burning sun, gives the animal the wrong food or forgets the water, which means he is not up to the task of keeping animals.

Some children will torment animals because they want to see what, for example, a fly will do with its wings torn out. They experiment with animals as if they were inanimate objects. The rolled up hedgehog resembled a ball — and the six-year-old girl played football with it! Her mother was inconsolable. Scolding or spanking is usually not a suitable method of making the child aware of its cruelty. Mother's sad face, her compassion for the tormented animal and, above all, careful explanation, as well as telling stories which awaken a respect for life — these are effective means of making the child aware of animals as fellow living creatures.

Some children develop into young animal doctors. An eight-year-old brought home from his holidays a toad whose back was one big wound because of a heath-fire. Daily, for a whole winter, the boy dusted the toad's back with Dermatol. When spring came, he was able to let it go in the woods, healed and well cared for. Later on, this boy also managed to rear fledglings which the neighbouring children used to bring to him. Now he is grown up, his work is in the service of those of his fellow men who are maimed or suffering.

There is no substitute for observing animals, but a small piece of nature, closely observed, can create the perceptive qualities for bigger experiences later. If one cannot exercise one's observation on a Sunday walk in the local wood, neither will one experience anything by the sea or in the mountains. He who cannot see a woodpecker or a squirrel here, need not think he will see a starfish or a marmot there. He who does not know ordinary flowers, will not notice the rare ones.

A child can learn to be perceptive through the example of the perceptive adult. Two things can be effective: on the one hand, the true intensity and inner participation with which some in itself inconspicuous natural process is observed and impressively conveyed to the child; on the other hand, the power of the imagination which transforms the everyday into something extraordinary, and thus creates adventures which are effective because they act on the child as real experiences.

I must still have been very small when on an autumn walk my grandmother showed me how the fallen leaves on the path, wet with rain, changed back to earth. Some had only just fallen, others were already decayed with only the shape of the leaf still recognizable — a scrape with the sole of one's shoe and they turned to earth. A conversation on the transient followed.

Through the power of the imagination a normal walk can be made much more exciting and the stamina of the children strengthened. The thirst, hunger and heat of a summer hike are borne heroically, whilst 'the caravan toils laboriously through the grinding sand, deceived again and again by mirages, until finally the longed-for oasis comes into sight' — the café, in fact. How quickly the complaints of tired children come to an end on the long way home at night if the way 'passes through the territory of a hostile tribe and one has to be on continuous look-out for enemy scouts'. I can still remember today the wonderful colours of the crevasses and ice caves through which we were led by our aunt in the course of a difficult glacier walk, which picked its way through the back-yard, via the stairs to the wood-shed and through the scullery of our town apartment!

This peerless aunt of ours had thought of another especially impressive game by aid of which she gave us children — landlubbers that we were — an impression of the tides of the sea. From various journeys she had brought back masses of Atlantic seashells, oyster shells, razor shells, whelks, starfish and seaweed. Now she was the rising tide and advanced roaring further and further into the room, going back only a little after each advance. And each time she advanced she spread on the floor handfuls of her sea-treasures which we tried to gather rapidly into baskets — always being chased by the next incoming wave. Soon however, our aunt changed it to the ebbing tide and took her treasures back with her into the 'sea'. Thus events of nature can be played — after the child's own experience or simply out of the imagination.

Repeating his own experiences through play gives the child the chance to assimilate them properly, and prepares him for new ones. Small children also appreciate it enormously if their own experiences are retold to them, where possible with illustrations. One mother I know has made wall-hangings for her three children: on the one is their own house, the garden, the flowers and the family; the second shows their holiday house in the Black Forest, the forested heights, the neighbour with her children and her cattle; and finally, on the third, can be seen the Alps, the jagged Swiss mountains which the family also visits each year. The children contemplate their wall-hangings every evening and are reminded of lovely experiences.

Memories and often-told stories are kept alive by means of the 'treasure box', which in one form or another belongs in every nursery. There are to be found all those natural playthings which were thought worthy of taking home during the course of the year, and now serve for imaginative games and the reliving of memorable experiences. What can be found in such a box? Smooth colourful pebbles from the beach, pieces of pink granite from Scotland, seashells, snailshells, chestnuts, a piece of drift-wood like a man, acorns, a bit of deer antler, a couple of cow's teeth and a dried-out tree fungus, a few fossils, a stone with calcite or quartz crystals, a piece of amber, a bit of thistle-down. Sometimes such a piece can turn into a lifelong companion and silently accompany the owner from one desk drawer to the next — where again and again it calls up the memory of a long lost paradise, until he finally sets out and travels to 'that place' with his own children.

Unsuitable for collecting, created only for the moment, sometimes gone in an hour — at most after a few days — the short-lived natural playthings tenaciously maintain their place in life — some have already done so for thousands of years! Who was it that bound up the first wreath of flowers? Which shepherd cut the first willow-pipe? Where was it that a mother first put a rattling seedpod into her child's hands to play with? Little baskets, helmets and skirts made out of reeds, blowpipes out of stalks, shelters from sun or rain out of gigantic leaves — ancient, and yet every time completely fresh and new — transient, yet with the promise of return!

The short-lived toys of nature accompany the child throughout the year: reed-pipes made from wild chervil at Easter; long water pipes and fountains made by joining dandelion stalks; castles and houses made by piling up mounds of freshly cut grass; lovely, fairy-like dolls' tea-parties made from all kinds of blossoms and plants. Then the little figures hidden away inside plants have to come to light: dolls' faces are picked out of mallow buds; poppy blooms turned down to make ladies with ruffs. Stalks and fruits serve to make all kinds of animals and birds. With autumn come chestnut animals, necklaces made of rowan berries and, finally, turnip lanterns. In the winter, there are potato-dolls, and bright orange-peel can be transformed into little baskets, snakes, crowns, little monkeys, and masks which shrink to strange wizened faces within a few days. In the woods, where no snow has fallen, a little dwarf's house can be erected from moss and twigs — with a proper garden-fence around it — and in the evening, the song of the rose-petal boat reminds the children of the flower games of the summer:

A ship I saw a-sailing,
A ship so wondrous fair
The crew were difficult to see,
So small were they, all there.
The bow was made of rose-petals,
The mast was a rose's thorn;
A beetle stood at the steering-helm,
And a beetle at the stern.
Lovely four-winged dragonflies,
Rocked to the wavelets' measure,
Travelled as the passengers
And had the greatest pleasure.
O dear good evening breeze,
Blow only sweet and low
Else the ship will sink with man and mouse,
And all the joy will go.

Anon.

The Human World

What applies to all the child's surroundings described so far must be said with special emphasis in relation to its human environment: It is impossible for a child to find its way into human society if it does not have the opportunity, from the earliest age, of growing into it through play and imitation. Everyone today has read publications on the developmental disturbances that appear in hospitalized children. They are looked after with impeccable hygiene, but, having no stimuli and no examples to follow, they do not develop properly; they become spiritually and physically backward and, after a certain length of time in such an institution, are lost to normal development. I was particularly impressed by a report on two Italian children's homes which I read in an illustrated magazine over ten years ago. One of them, an excellently run private home, took in children from wealthy families, for whom only the best was good enough for their babies. The well-trained staff worked impeccably, yet with all the children the typical developmental disturbances of hospitalization were noted. The second home, which was part of a women's prison, was set up to care for the babies of convicted mothers. — Babies from just those circles where in normal life one expects to meet neglected, backward children. Here each child was cared for by its mother, who for this purpose was allowed to enter the children's home for a short time each day, and for whom these times with her child meant the only joy and variation in the routine of prison life. In contrast to the expensive establishment, this children's home was full of splendid children. It was the conspicuous difference in the development of the children in the two homes that prompted a doctor to write the report. The personal interest of the nurse, her caressing and fondling, make the child thrive. In recognition of this fact, the nurses in some Russian children's homes (I don't know in how many) are forbidden to talk to one another while they are tending a child; each one must speak and play exclusively with the child she is tending at the time. They have learned the importance of talking to children. To prevent the harmful effects of passing a child from one person to another there was a custom in the Municipal Children's Home of Lörrach, when I was training in baby care, that each child was looked after by its own particular nurse or trainee. Thus one could hear: 'Angela, your Johnny is crying!' and Angela had to go and see.

The person who is most intensively concerned with the child in its first year holds a key position; it is up to that person to prepare the child for living among its fellow human beings. To make up later what has been neglected in the first year is one of the great and arduous tasks of curative education. What every loving mother, aunt, grandmother or elder sister manages without specialist knowledge during the first year, requires at a later stage great and devoted commitment, work and powers of soul on the part of carefully trained people, which can never be adequately recompensed.

As soon as the child lifts its little head and looks round, it wants to see *everything*. As soon as it can totter along behind the adult it wants to *touch* everything, and soon also *do* everything. At the time, this can be pure horror: the chair is massaged with cream, the piano washed, the coffeegrounds tipped into the soup, the glue into the aquarium, and the paint-thinner into the washing machine — all in the famous unguarded moment! At this stage, the infant in the kitchen or work-room is a kind of natural-disaster — not every infant, but many! One of my sons, who at this age could play for hours with two pins without doing himself any harm, only turned into a problem when, at the age of three, he started knotting and tying all available strings, laces and ribbons, together with furniture and toys, into one big tangle. This nerve-racking game remained his daily exercise for some time, and my leisure time occupation.

Quite soon the infant can join in with the adults in their work: with a small broom, a mop and a duster he helps Mother clean the house. Spoons can be dried at an early age, and many a four-year-old already does all the drying up. If Father is repairing the car, it is advisable to cover the hammer our young apprentice is holding with a rubber tube, or to give him a rubber hammer in the first place. Depending on where one lives, it is possible to send even the youngest shopping, equipped with a small rucksack or basket. A great deal of the interesting and exciting house and handiwork that children grow into through play is nowadays done with machines. It is therefore all the more important not to deny children the chance to participate in as much of it as possible.

In the kindergarten of the 'Lebenshilfe' in Völklingen, the children are always allowed to watch and help with the cooking of lunch. This may certainly make the work of the cooks more difficult, but for the children it is a real help for life.

I shall never forget a scene from a cultural film on Burma in which a family is rowing along a river in its houseboat. A small child stands beside his mother, his tiny hands holding on to the oar, so that its rhythm is absorbed by his whole being.

The imitative games of children can become unbeliev-

ably troublesome! The things that I alone have experienced!
. . . Some concrete was being laid for foundations; my
small sons smuggled some of the concrete away in their
coat pockets and proceeded to lay it in the nests in
Grandmother's henhouse. The electrician is busy in the
house; not only does there appear a totally senseless, but
deep slit in the wall of the boys' room, but our two-year-old
takes a screwdriver to bed for his afternoon rest and during
that time dismantles a light-switch. Without technically
highly trained guardian-angels, none of my sons would be
alive now — and I am not saying that as a joke!

*

Not only the work they see being done, but many other
things children want to learn, imitate and try out with their
whole person. Into whom and what will a small child not
turn itself to discover the manifoldness of life! There are
girls who for a time want to be boys, boys who in turn want
to be girls, and who dress and behave accordingly. This can
happen for no obvious reason, or there can be a definite
cause for the transformation.

Once an excited neighbour rang at the door: for the
second time in two days the three-and-a-half-year-old had
run in front of his car and only sudden braking had saved the
worst. When the neighbour had gone, the mother looked
around for her son — ah, he had crept into the corner under
the table, whence he only came back into the daylight after
an hour. But then for two days he refused to leave the house
in case he met the neighbours who had witnessed his folly.
Finally he thought of a solution: 'Make my hair different
and give me another name, so that no one will know me', he
demanded. Fine! His mother tied two red ribbons into his
blond hair and called him Mary. Later he preferred to be
called Angela, after his older friend, but he remained a girl
for several months. To a ticket inspector on a train who

asked him in a friendly way: 'What's your name, son?' he answered darkly: 'I'm a girl!'

For several weeks one small boy turned into a dog, and his plate had to be put on the floor — he was, however, a nice, tame and well-behaved dog, who went obediently on the lead. Of his own accord he turned back into a human child.

Here we are right into play-acting. It became more serious when, day after day, a small girl in a kindergarten turned into a dog, whereupon the other children also followed her example. On many days the activity of the teacher was restricted to 'training' the 'dogs' — at most little scenes with dogs could be performed. She began to look for the cause of the problem: all the 'dogs' were well-behaved and good-natured except for the original one; this one growled and did not want to behave. When the other 'dogs' gradually turned back into children this one remained a 'dog'. The teacher visited the parents and found a well cared-for semi-detached house, where the girl, an only child, had to spend her time in her room. The dog, however, which had joined the family a few months previously, was allowed to be everywhere, even on the sofa and the chairs. The teacher succeeded in making the parents aware of the desperate and justifiable jealousy of the child, and they succeeded in finding a solution: they gave their daughter the task of feeding the dog and thus clearly made it subordinate to her. Now she was able to give up her role as a dog.

I knew two sisters who transformed themselves, Sunday after Sunday. The younger one always changed into the Princess, the older into the Prince or the Governess — depending on what was necessary. Other parts were those of the monkey and his keeper. The father's veto, however, put an end to that; the part of the monkey in the long run really went beyond the strength of the youngest daughter.

Occasionally the mother of several daughters is visited by three 'princesses, struck by poverty, who have to go into service among strangers, not to die of hunger'. When the mother then says to one of them: 'Dear Princess, you can clean out my daughter's bird cage, then you can eat lunch with us in place of my daughter!' the princess is somewhat embarrassed by this suggestion, for perhaps it was just from the bird cage that she wanted to escape into the role of princess!

For two days a little boy became a devil. For dressing up, it was sufficient to fix a piece of hose on to the back of his shorts — the devil's tail! He dipped this tail into the cleaning-bucket and went dripping round the room; he screamed excessively, and 'played the devil' in every possible way. Then the little fellow suddenly became doubtful and he approached his mother: 'Now I would rather be an angel!' And so he was.

In this way, acting a part can often help to overcome problems as they occur in growing up. At four or five years of age, one little girl started having tantrums and would fling herself about the room in rages. Her older sister, not liking this development, told her the story of Rumpelstiltskin. Then they acted the fairy-tale. Once the little sister had played the part of Rumpelstiltskin with complete absorption, her need for choleric outbreaks was satisfied; only very rarely and on really worthwhile occasions did they ever recur.

Where a problem appears in the development of a child, or even a group of children, it is in many cases better to present the fault quite clearly in caricature in a play, rather than try to achieve anything by reason and persuasion. By giving a child a wisely chosen role to play, one can often reach parts of its being that are inaccessible to any other influence. Many a teacher has created a willingness to learn in an obdurate class, or corrected an unfortunate development through a performance.

The child enters into another important experience when play-acting. A performance, especially written for the occasion, or perhaps already to hand, put on the stage (or the garden lawn) to celebrate a special occasion for well-loved people, such as grandparents, gives them great pleasure. This pleasure comes as the crowning reward for the carefully prepared presentation and heightens the joy of the children; it enriches them with the experience that giving joy is the surest way of achieving it.

Thus the playing of parts is very important, and it is up to us to support and facilitate this. Let us accordingly always give something to our children or godchildren for their 'theatre-trunk' or 'dressing-up-drawer'. A discarded lace dress, an old top-hat, a piece of beautiful red material for a royal cloak, a piece of gold lamé, some cord and that old blue curtain, cast off costume jewellery — let us be ready at any time to cater for further props: a knight's breastplate can be made from old cardboard boxes with a stapler; a nurse's cap may be urgently needed when the dolls have fallen ill, or even if one is allowed to take the odd thing to Father when he is ill in bed — for a nurse such service is her *raison d'être*, whereas a little daughter can become tired of it.

With these things the same applies as it does so often with toys: he gives doubly, who gives immediately. Quite suddenly something may be needed — an Indian headdress, a robber's beard, a crown. Let us leave the pyjamas unironed this time, and make instead a beard from the bits of hemp left in Father's work cupboard. The pyjamas are forgotten. The game of robbers shines into the future as one of the highlights of childhood.

*

51

But there is one thing that is not effectively overcome by the playing of parts, even if they are continually repeated: the aggressive instinct. A widespread contemporary phenomenon, which is wrongly taken to be the necessary working off of these instincts, is described in the following extract from an article by the television editor Margie Lucas[8]:

Several families live in the house where I do: a doctor, a judge, an advertising executive, a hotel proprietor; a good cross-section of the upper middle class, not at all old fashioned or stolid. They all have children. The children play with one another in the courtyard or the garden. It sounds like this: — 'Hey you, watch it!' — 'Hands up!' — 'Bang, bang, bang!' — 'Ah-h-h! Mummy! He hit me!' 'Hands up! And make it quick!', — 'Tr-r-r-r-. . .' (this is supposed to be a machine-gun) 'You dare . . . you'll get it!' — 'Now you be the gangster and I'll be the sheriff . . . and you stick the knife in my stomach — no, deeper — deeper, you idiot! And then I shoot — no you have to run first — run!' — 'Bang!' — 'Ah-h-h-h!' —. And this carries on for hour after hour.

In the evening they sit in front of the television. One thriller and then another; in between, a Western. Murder and manslaughter; someone doubles up in pain, screams; one is wounded, several dead . . . The sweet darlings sit there, breathless, with craning necks; then they go to sleep and lie rosy and snug in their beds, and the next day it starts all over again: 'Ah!' — 'Bang!' — 'I'm going to . . . — you've got to . . . then I'll . . . Tr-r-r-r-!'

'Well, those are the natural aggressions, the children have to work them off. You don't understand anything of child-psychology . . .'

Yes, that's probably true.

The parents accordingly watch with radiant smiles from their flower decorated balconies how their little angels threaten and shout at each other, and shoot one another with their cute toy pistols . . . 'The natural instincts have to be taken into account; we even once read a book by Freud and, after all, we are enlightened people, aren't we?'. . .

If 'bang — bang' and 'tr-r-r-r!' were of the least value in working off the aggressive instincts, then these games should have a calming effect — another day, a different game would surely indicate the result of the 'cure'. But nothing of the sort happens; 'bang — bang!' and 'tr-r-r-r!' continue to fill the other days. So it is of no use. It is merely an imitative game. But what *is* of use? There is a saying: 'The devil makes use of idle hands'. That is just it. The recipe is as old as man himself. Work is the cure; exertion, application of one's own strength. Not everyone has the chance, but work in the fields, garden work, digging holes, chopping wood, carrying coals, rolling the lawn, iugging stones are all useful in this respect. It is a wise grandmother who does not let the gardener dig up the old espalier since two wild grandchildren are expected in the near future. If the children are small enough, such a tree is sufficient for the aggression of one to two weeks.

In his book about his memories of youth[9], Wilhelm von Kügelgen describes one of those games which are suitable for letting children try out their own strength.

One fine afternoon [Caspar David] Friedrich suggested to us children a special amusement, namely to erect a tower right in the water. Enthusiastically wading through the shallow stream we heaved the stones for building it. Friedrich, standing in the water like a long-legged heron, stacked them all into a pyramid or pillar which soon rose out of the water to the height of a man. . . .

With this, however, the fun was not finished, but had only just begun. It was not the idea to allow either time or naughty boys the honour of destroying Friedrich's work of art — we would rather do this ourselves — and everyone got into the water . . . and gathered up stones from the bottom.

A marvellous bombardment now began, and unspeakable enjoyment, for there is a great and basic delight in destruction for everyone. The missiles, dispatched by sturdy hands, beat from all sides against the monument and crashed back into the water together with the shattered parts of the ruin. The water spurted in many rivulets round the dark edifice, forming cascades and clouds of spray in which sparkled the rays of the evening sun, until the destruction was complete.

Such games are still possible in many areas today, and an excursion can be made more effective and memorable by this type of game than by reaching a famous place. At home, building and destroying great towers made from all available building blocks affords similar enjoyment on an indoor scale. Unfortunately many houses are now built with such poor sound-proofing that even this game is often considered a nuisance.

How can we help our town children towards activities for which they have to use their physical strength? Although in existence for decades and used in many countries, the 'adventure-playground' is still a rarity and generally unknown. Just as an open-air swimming pool, supervised by an attendant, is a substitute for the natural opportunities for swimming afforded by rivers, lakes or the sea, in the same way the adventure-playground serves as a substitute for the wasteland and junk yards which are no longer available to city children. On a small scale, children can dig caves and build houses, they can light fires, saw, hammer and paint. Someone is in charge. He distributes the tools and bits of advice, prevents the children from doing too dangerous things, protects the weak ones and represents his playground in the local area.

On such playgrounds children from high-rise blocks come face to face with the elements. Together with children from over-protected environments they can test their strength on thick wooden logs and six-inch nails. Single children can learn social behaviour, timid ones gain self-confidence. Those who have been neglected or deprived find attention, praise and encouragement. They all learn how to use tools and develop a feeling for different materials. They overcome anxieties, learn to assess hazards and to take calculated risks. With a great sense of responsibility, a group of foreign workers' children take care of the much-loved pony of their adventure-playground in Basle. This task carries great honour and gives these children a certain prestige.

Another possibility for working off accumulated aggressive or destructive urges is offered by healthy physical exercise, such as swimming, winter sports, gymnastics, wrestling or riding. Yet it will always remain the responsibility of the parents to protect gifted children from the ambitions of the trainers and their commercially interested backers. Whatever sport one chooses, the favourite game that dominates the days of one's childhood and youth can be a decisive influence in life.

The events recorded in the following extract from Lincoln Steffens[7] happened nearly a hundred years ago.

My life on horseback from the age of eight to fifteen was a happy one, free, independent, full of romance, adventure, and learning, of a sort. Whether my father had any theories about it or was moved only by my prayers I do not know. But he did have some ideas . . .

I had begun about that time to play boys' games: marbles, tops, baseball, football, and I can see now my father stopping on his way home to watch us. He used to wag his head; he said nothing to me, but I knew he did not like those games. I think now that he thought there was some gambling in them, and he had reason to dread gambling. It was a vice that hung over from the mining days in California, and the new businessmen were against it . . . My father had had to discharge a favorite bookkeeper on account of his heavy play at the gaming-tables. He may have given me the pony to keep me from gambling games or to get me up off the streets and out into the country. There was another result, however, which he did not foresee. After that blessed pony loped into my life, I never played those trading games which, as I see them now, are the leads not merely to gambling but to business. For there goes on among boys an active trade in marbles, tops, knives, and all the other tools and properties of boyhood. A born trader finds himself in them, and the others learn to like to trade. My theory is that those games are the first lessons in business: they cultivate the instinct to beat the other fellows on 'Change and so quicken their predatory wits. Desirable or no, I never got that training; I never had any interest in, I have always had a distaste for, business, and this my father did not intend. I remember how disappointed he was later when he offered to stay in his business till I could succeed him and I rejected the 'great opportunity' with quick scorn — 'Business! Never.'

My pony carried me away not only from business but from the herd also and the herding habits of mind. This tendency of the human animal to think what others think, say what the mob says, do what the leaders do or command, and, generally, go with the crowd, is drilled in deep at school, where the playground has its fashions, laws, customs and tyrannies just as Main Street has. I missed that. I never played 'follow the leader', never submitted to the ideals and the discipline of the campus or, for that matter, of the faculty; and so, ever since, I have been able to buy stocks during a panic, sell when the public was buying; I could not always face, but I could turn my back on, public opinion. I think I learned this when, as a boy on horseback, my interest was not in the campus; it was beyond it . . .

*

Living with one's fellow men is something that has to be learnt. For some people it is easier, for others more difficult. Circumstances will sometimes be favourable for getting on well together, at other times not so favourable — occasionally sacrifices have to be made to keep the peace. Nasty surprises await the person who does not know with whom he is dealing.

Team games, indoor or outdoor, in fact any games that require a number of people, foster the abilities and the understanding for life in human society — above all, the realization that one needs the others. It is impossible to play these games alone. How can one hide oneself from oneself, or catch oneself? Even playing one's right hand against the left in a board-game is not really so exciting.

It is necessary, then, to find friends; and already the child has to learn to behave in such a manner that the others want to play with him. He learns either to give way, or to lead; in the best circumstances both. It is to be hoped he also learns the difficult art of losing! There are of course some children naturally gifted with the art of losing game after game and still remaining in the best of tempers — throughout a whole evening! These are the ones who make easy contact, for whom the company is more important and interesting than winning a game. There are others who have to be helped in every way so that they do not lose their tempers every time their luck fails, and thus become spoilsports. One can make it clear to them what a noble art it is to lose with grace; but above all one should teach them to distinguish between important and unimportant things — and not, for example, to lose a friend for the sake of a game.

Once the spell is broken and our child plays with the others, it acquires a whole series of abilities which will give it stability in life.

Judging character is one thing that is practised. With 'hide-and-seek' it depends very much on who is searching; one always falls for the trick with the house corner, whereas another moves around so quickly that a very good hiding-place is needed to escape detection. Where two leaders are allowed to choose their teams alternately from a crowd of children, precise judgments are made and the situation cleverly weighed up, until finally the small and clumsy ones are also distributed equally among both teams. Not only is there practice in judging each one by his capabilities and using him accordingly: 'You're quick and thin, you go as a scout — you're so strong, you guard the prisoners!'; the lesser possibilities of the small and weak ones are also taken into consideration and used.

In the Russian kolkhoz village the children divide themselves into two teams on the basis of self-judgment. I follow the description of Wladimir Ssolouchin[10]:

These Russian children form pairs, always two of equal strength. Each pair thinks of two words which also correspond. For example, one is the gate, the other the fence. One a stable, the other a barn. Then they step in front of the two captains who have been chosen earlier and who are, of course, also of equal strength. They ask the one: 'Do you want gate or fence?' 'Gate' he may answer, and the boy who has chosen 'gate' will go and stand in his team and the boy who is 'fence' goes to the other side. Thus pair after pair go to the captains and ask the one, then the other:

'Nail or horseshoe?'
'Plough or harrow?'
'Forest or river?'

The girls choose more delicate symbols:

'Lilac or elderberry?'
'Cornflower or forget-me-not?'
'Red or blue?'

The final result is the same as with our more authoritarian procedure: in the end two equally strong groups stand facing one another. Only the choosing of the teams in the kolkhoz is already an exciting game in itself.

Years ago, five brothers and sisters founded a 'Society for the Promotion of Virtues' which lasted about two years. It was the idea of a sixth form boy who lived in the house as a lodger. The eldest sister was also in the lower sixth. Amid great hilarity, the statutes were drawn up and the office bearers and functionaries appointed. The thirteen-year-old brother was made chairman of the board, and had little to do (or say!). The boarder became the general secretary, since he was thought to have the necessary neutrality and authority, in the case of quarrels, in not belonging to the family. The treasurer was the eldest sister. It was also her task to check that before meal-times all hands were spotlessly clean. The sixteen-year-old sister was welfare and also sports official. The ten-year-old brother was the society's man-servant and the youngest sister of eight was listed as *the* proper member. The parents and their mother's helper were appointed honorary members, and this honour put them five pence out of pocket per month. The others paid half that amount.

The aims of the society were simple and noble: the cultivation of order and cleanliness, decent behaviour and comradeship. The pursuit of knowledge was also quoted as an aim. Monetary fines were levied on any breaches of conduct: spots on the tablecloth, dirty hands, untidy books, tyrannizing over one's brothers or sisters, false pretences, putting on a martyred air, misuse of authority. Good deeds were praised, and sometimes even rewarded — for example, getting rid of daddy long-legs. Cultural events formed a part of the society's programme. Musical presentations alternated with the theatre; Schiller's *The Glove* was performed in the spacious hall — the 'welfare officer' as the lion was most impressive — as well as Goethe's *The Fisherman*. A lecture on mice broadened the members' knowledge.

Since there is no getting away from the fact that not only the small and the clumsy, but also the mentally and physically handicapped are amongst our fellow men, it is not right to want to hide their existence from normal healthy children. Indeed, children are often more at ease with them than some adults, and they invent games which include their handicapped playmate. Such a game is described in a short story by Clara Viebig[11]:

Dear God, what a poor specimen of a child was Christoph Nepomuk! He had a hump on his back and a hump on his front;

his thin, wobbly legs could hardly carry his body, and in between his raised shoulders rested a large head with a wizened old face . . . Around the mouth there were deep wrinkles, oh, and the big black eyes did not look out with child-like joy . . . into the world. What use was it to Christoph Nepomuk that he had two beautiful saints as namesakes? — 'A miserable little wretch' the people said.

For the mother, who was widowed early, and had to earn her sparse living by strenuous day-labour, the child was a heavy burden. The whole day she had to leave him on his own, and on Sunday she lit a thin candle under the picture of the Holy Virgin in the chapel on the hill: 'Holy Mother of God, pray for us! Holy Mother of God, let him soon be among the angels!' meaning the 'miserable little wretch'.

On nice, sunny days the lonely little chap dragged himself over to the neighbouring house where he called out his faithful playmates, Toni and Josepha.

The two children took the little cripple between them and carried him a bit further up to the green patch of grass where bugloss flowered, cowslips and lady smock, buttercups and wild roses.

There the three sat down. Josepha picked some of the yellow flowers, joined them by the stems and made a long chain which she hung round the neck of the wretched little one. 'Now you're beautiful, little wretch', she said, 'now let's play at processions!'

Those were happy hours for Christoph Nepomuk! He sat in the warm sunlight on the soft grass and played 'Saint Christopher'. Toni and Josepha moved past him with measured steps, carrying yellow flowers instead of candles; they babbled and crossed themselves, curtsied and prayed: 'Holy Saint Christopher, pray for us! Holy Saint Christopher, let the little wretch soon join the angels!'

And the 'little wretch' nodded blithely with his head; it was so beautiful!

Two things can be seen in this short episode: first, the procession game, originating in church ceremony, where, in this case, the person who plays Saint Christopher is without embarrassment at the same time the subject of the supplication which he is called upon to grant. Moreover, it indicates how naturally children can include a handicapped companion in their games.

I heard that in a certain school the previous year's first class always welcomed the next group of members of the school with a small celebration. Finally, a round dance was performed and then the new ones were invited: 'Come and dance with us!' Shyly the children remained standing with their mothers; only one stepped forward, a thalidomide child with no arms! The teacher and the parents held their breath — but the children took the child right and left by his coat and happily started dancing.

Jacques Lusseyran, who lost his eyesight at the age of eight, writes in his wonderful autobiography *And There Was Light*[12]:

> What about running? I couldn't do without it, yet running by myself was impossible. I had to find a team-mate of my own age, and this was easy. People are always wrong in thinking that most children are not obliging, and don't like cluttering up their games with someone whom adults call an invalid. I assure you that for children there are no invalids. The bright boys hate the stupid ones, and the enterprising run from the cowards. It is as simple as that. Neither eyes nor legs have anything to do with it.
>
> No boy in Juvardeil ever refused me his hand or arm or gave it grudgingly. Sometimes they even bickered to see which one should have the right to hold me by the shoulder and run with me as fast as our legs could carry us . . .

Wherever a handicapped child appears in a circle of children, one should try to arrange it so that occasionally a game is included in which he can also join. For example the game 'Tip', which is suitable for all ages. I recommend it highly for these occasions:

61

On a table there are placed lots of little things to nibble: raisins, nuts, biscuits, cherries, chocolate, perhaps a tiny glass of juice, and so forth. Someone goes out and the others decide which piece is to be 'tip'. The first person comes back in and begins to gather up piece after piece until he picks up the one designated 'tip'. Then he has to stop — perhaps already at the first attempt! All things taken away are replaced and the next one goes out.

Here everyone has an equal chance and consideration for the handicapped demands no further sacrifice. In playing hide-and-seek and lotto, for example, children of their own free will let the weaker ones win from time to time, although this sometimes has to be helped along a bit.

If a large number of people already learn in their childhood to consider the rights of those who are weaker, and to arrange their games in such a manner that no one has to be excluded, then this can be seen as a contribution to world peace in the long run. Where there are no suppressed minorities embittered by suffering, and no career-people who 'walk over them', a great deal is already won; depending on the example set, one way or the other can already be taken in the imitative games of early childhood.

It is in the strict separation of those who are different, less gifted, weaker, that the problem of streaming lies. In the 'top stream' classes we are breeding members of a ruling class who have neither practised nor even learned to know social attitudes and social responsibility in their youth. Do we really want that?

It is certainly better if there is a colourful mixture, where every child has the opportunity of learning how to get on with stronger and weaker ones, rougher and gentler ones, more daring and more timid ones, how to live with other people, and thus acquires the foundations for psychology, sociology and diplomacy. In Waldorf schools mixed ability classes are the rule. Neither the highly gifted nor the less gifted are segregated from their age group; only those in need of special attention are helped in extra classes.

*

It is not only by acting different roles himself, playing games with others that the child gradually learns the human world by imitation. Another possibility is that children do not directly act everything and take on each part themselves, but use toy models to imitate what happens around them and moves them. Throughout the world, and from very ancient times, games are known that no more exclude the sphere of religious ceremonies than the actual acting games and may in fact have originated there (or in the realm of magic). In Germany one could on occasions buy dolls and all the apparatus especially for re-enacting the Mass: priests, monks, nuns and novices of all types. Then there are shepherds and their flocks; farms with people, animals and machines; the inevitable armies or toy soldiers of all times; dolls' houses with whole families; carters with horses and wagons; crusaders with fine castles; Noah's Ark with man and animals — two of every kind; all types of cars, with and without chauffeurs; trains, ships, aircraft. The child plays at the 'human world' with all these toys, some of which leave room for the imagination, some hardly any.

Some children have such a strong and creative imagination that they can create and use all the props necessary for their games out of absolutely nothing. Invisible tills ring and empty hands measure out sugar and salt, so that it is unbelievable to watch. I have experienced several children coming up to me smiling broadly and offering their open or carefully cupped hands: 'Here is a present for you!' or 'I have brought you something!' We do well if we ask for a detailed description of the gift, so that we can imagine it and receive it with due thanks, and treat it carefully for such time as it exists in the imagination of the child: we lay invisible pieces of jewellery in front of the mirror; we eat the imaginary cake and find it delicious; we put the invisible nest full of fledglings on the window-sill 'so that the mother can feed them'.

Such games of the imagination further the mobility of mind and the powers of expression. It also happens, of course, that the imagination can raise fear and terror. Here too, it is best to treat it seriously and do something to overcome it. One day I came into my kitchen to find both my sons cowering in front of the cupboard: 'Mother, there is a wolf under the table!' Immediately I reached for one of Father's hiking-boots, aimed, and flung it under the table with great noise. 'There, now the wolf is dead.' Quite satisfied, my sons continued playing and forgot the wolf, alive or dead.

Not every imaginary terror can be allayed this easily. Occasionally an excorcism can help. After we had read together the second scene in the study from *Faust*, where the poodle turns into a wandering scholar after the excorcism, and then cannot leave the room because of the pentagram, — a scene enormously popular with children — the most imaginative of my sons wanted to know how a pentagram is drawn. He proceeded to learn it and then drew it all over his bed and the walls of his room as a protection against all kinds of spectres.

It is unnecessary to worry about such occurrences. They will pass on their own. The phase of games of unlimited imagination passes too. Where at first a simple building block was enough to represent a man, a cow, a loaf of bread, gradually greater distinction — even absolutely clear definition — is demanded of these symbols. It is funny to observe how perhaps an eye or an ear which has never been missed before is suddenly drawn on to a wooden animal or a cloth doll.

The small-size models are made of the most varied materials. Gold and precious stones formed the toys of the children of nobility; straw and rags the dolls of the poor; whale- and fishbone those of Eskimo-children. Out of the clay in the pit in which he is kept prisoner by the Tartars, the 'prisoner in the Caucasus' (Tolstoy) makes small dolls and throws them out to the village elder's little daughter, who later helps him to escape. Mother's supply of old rags provided material for a cow, a goat and a very fat pig for a little girl who had got to know these animals in her holidays, but had unfortunately not been able to take them home. Her mother assured me that her daughter completed the three large rag-animals very naturalistically and had played a lot with them.

Wood, metals, and recently, plastic are the chief materials used, but here follow two specially impressive examples of imaginative discovery through models made of paper and clay or wax. The first again comes from Wilhelm von Kügelgen[9]:

The most enjoyable thing that Senff [the tutor] taught us was the art of folding certain triangular figures out of paper, otherwise known as crows. In making them, the last fold was so difficult that it could not be taught; it was rather a case of being lucky enough to achieve a certain intellectual understanding, or in other words, the scales had to fall from one's eyes before it was possible to complete the most carefully prepared crow by this last creative fold. 'Can you do the last fold yet?' — for a long time that was the most burning question of the day amongst us. . .

Meanwhile, these paper figures were supposed to represent nothing less than crows — with which one can't really do anything — but rather soldiers, which our obedient imagination also willingly let them be . . . Indeed, we were so enthusiastically involved with these angular little figures, that

65

they appeared far more natural to us than those leaden idiots, which looked as if they had just escaped from a herbarium. Through differences in the colour of the paper and small differences of fold, we could represent all different military types, even cavalry, as Senff had discovered that these soldiers could be changed and stretched in such a way through a highly ingenious final manipulation, that they . . . now looked just as much like horses as they had before like men. One only had to sit the infantry on them.

At Christmas, after the giving of presents, the tutor led the houseparty into a large room at the back of the house:

. . . and here on the floor Senff had constructed the town of Constantinople out of small paper houses, palaces, mosques. Nothing could have been more neatly made than this paper town. Thickly spread white sand indicated the land, blue sand the sea, which was alive with little ships.

After Senff had given a brief description of the most prominent spots, he remarked that Constantinople often used to burn down, and with that he lit a touch paper under the first house in the suburb of Pera. Soon the flames broke out, jumped to the next house, then the whole street, branching away into other streets, leaping into the wells, which were filled with paraffin, and spread through the whole city. Finally the Seraglio caught alight, and its countless turrets burst apart like miniature fireworks, bringing the performance to a sensational end.

Perhaps at this point the reader thinks what a pity it was that the skilful tutor's painstaking work was simply destroyed like that. But such sacrifices by a teacher are seeds which soon begin to sprout, and Kügelgen continues:

Naturally we were eager to copy everything, from the small lights made of nutshells to the little ships and paper buildings. The fortresses and towns which up till then . . . had only been drawn as groundplans for our games, now rose in all dimensions, and came by all kinds of knowledge and skill.

Had the ingenious tutor just left the town, built with so much love, to his charges to play with, then the result would have been watered down; the initial delight would have given way to familiarity, and one after another the houses and palaces would have been played with until forgotten, finally ending up in the fire. But in this way the sacrifice of the tutor metamorphosed into the creative endeavours of the children.

The second example is from a book by Helene Christaller[13], written for the children of her daughter, who died young:

The children were playing in the garden. They had discovered a marvellous game. Outside the village there was a clay pit, and from there they had fetched their little cart filled with clay, and were creating man and animal as the Creator did at the beginning of the world. Walter had modelled a whole town from clay, with a church, a school, an inn, a well and a bakery. In between these he stuck green, bushy twigs as trees. Trudel made animals: cows with calves, cats and dogs. Erika had made a small nest with four clay eggs in it and a bird on top. Elsa, however, tried her hand at human beings. The children looked like piglets, covered from top to toe with clay, yet they were glowing with the pleasure of creating something, and finally decided that all they had made was very good. This game continued until one morning the clay was frozen hard. So Father brought home a few tablets of reddy-brown modelling wax as a substitute. With this the figures could be formed even more beautifully than with clay. Only, unfortunately it was not inexhaustible.

From that time on, the word 'wax' stood at the top of each list of wishes. Sometimes even more urgently: 'lots of wax'. And later black wax was wanted besides the reddy-brown, to make expressive hair and black horses and dogs.

At first, various different games were played with the wax.

Adam and Eve in Paradise with all the animals, then Noah's Ark.

Another time Nero appeared with many slaves, the circus, wild animals and Christians who were persecuted and tortured. A giant lion, made very real-looking by Trude, had a stomach which would open, so that it could also really eat up the pretty Christian girl with long black hair and white robe of innocence made of tissue paper. This gruesome scene was superseded by a flower-filled scene in heaven where there were angels big and small, the Virgin Mary and Saints.

After the eldest sister had read *The Last Days of Pompeii* and told the story to her brothers and sisters, the figures of this book came into being.

The wicked Egyptian sorcerer Arbaces, the blind Lydia, the beautiful Glamus . . . Walter made Mount Vesuvius erupt in flames, which nearly caused an accident. This was followed by *The Last of the Mohicans*, and the Indians were given beautiful headdresses with small feathers from the chicken-run.

Fairy-tales alternated with tales of the Germanic heroes. Greek Olympus with its gods and goddesses was superseded by the wonders of the Arabian Nights. The story of Joseph and his brothers was staged dramatically and the daughter of Jairus rose from her bed.

It is clear that a great deal of wax was needed for these games and that they remained inexhaustible for many years. But there came a point when they changed. Things were not dismantled anymore to begin anew, but the story of a whole town was developed, with many individual fates and fortunes, and whole family histories.

Underneath the fir trees in the garden there sprang up small houses and churches, theatres, a townhall, public baths, a prison, and parks — there was even a torture tower. The materials used for building the houses were bricks, slates, pieces of wood and all kinds of colourful bits and pieces from the rubbish. In honour of their mother, the town was called Ennepolis, and the children ruled the town as its four gods. God Walter was responsible for the constitution, the administration and the government, while the girls were more concerned with the fate of its people; they created new ones, set up marriages, founded schools, made dainty furniture and put many babies into the world.

This game continued for years, until at the age of thirteen the brother had to go to boarding school.

Time and space wise, such an extended game of human society is possible for only a very limited number of children today. But often a few, quickly modelled wax figures can help to lend vividness to a story or a recollection. So many forces are awakened in the child through modelling that clay and wax are among the most important play-things.

*

Possibly the reader may now think that, with all these many games the child allegedly needs, quite a lot is demanded of the parents. This is true. At least in cities, it demands a real effort if one wants to make it possible for children to conquer their surroundings through play. Happily, there are many parents for whom this seems worth the trouble, and who also manage to do it.

It is much less troublesome and exciting to teach the poor things to read already at kindergarten age. One does not need to get out of the armchair. The experts who lead the battle to teach children to read as early as possible, emphasize again and again how much more quiet and well-poised early readers are than those who play — just as if quietness and poise were desirable in children! Well, of course, the early readers can then read about all the things of which they have been deprived. But instead of assimilating experiences, they have information in their heads, and information is bound to be a quite inadequate substitute for experience.

The senses of these children are deprived of the manifold impressions which are needed to form them; and whilst the intellectual memory and the intellectual ability to learn are furthered intensively, other faculties and abilities atrophy and come badly off. This danger of atrophy when the intellect is developed *too early* particularly hinders the social abilities of such children.

Occasionally one meets the intellectual wonder child, who, although the youngest, is top of the class and masters everything without effort; — his schoolmates, however, do not want anything to do with him, and he is no more interested in them; he has no friends. It can remain like that throughout his life: he is always successful, passes all examinations brilliantly, but remains basically lonely. Although he is often asked for advice in technical matters, he is never consulted on the problems of life itself. This is not because he was top of the class, but because he was top *too early*, too young for that particular stage. If a child is top at the normal age of the class, he can act as its leader, or be an asset to it in a less obtrusive way. There are opportunities enough for him to learn *more* than his class mates.

An especially serious case of one-sided promotion of intelligence at the cost of the social abilities is evident in the American girl, Edith Stern. Various newspapers reported that she could read at the age of two, could play chess at three or four, as well as being at home in general history, and at five could do arithmetic and was conversant in philosophy. At sixteen a college employed her as a lecturer in higher mathematics. About this girl — her picture shows a dark-haired, podgy teenager with glasses — her father said that she had no feeling for the joys and sorrows of her fellow human beings, was cold and calculating, knew neither remorse nor compassion and never cried. The father, who had produced this intellectual wonder at such an early age, wanted to achieve the same for his son; but the mother did not permit it — the boy was to go to school like everyone else and become a normal child.

The mother is not alone in her objections. The warnings against too early an intellectual schooling for children accumulate — and they come from the most varied sources.

Professor Bruno Bettelheim is head of a 'school' for gifted, but emotionally disturbed children in Chicago. In his deeply disturbing book about all these — partly incurable — children who have been *made* ill, he tells of an autistic boy who had been intellectually pushed and put under great pressure from a very early age, among other things, through learning to read very young. *As a consequence* the development of his social faculties had 'naturally' suffered. When Bruno Bettelheim calls this result of too early reading 'natural', he knows what he is talking about. And we ought to believe him.

If it is true, that an over-early emphasis on the intellectual side frequently results in, or even causes, an underdevelopment of the social faculties, then we should think carefully about whether in these over-early readers a generation is not growing up, which, once we are old and can no longer be reckoned of any use, will not, in a very painless and humane way, just do away with us.

It will not be the intellectual abilities but the social faculties of human beings that will on the whole make it possible to live on this earth in the future; one should keep this in mind where young people are growing up. Computers can do calculations of every kind for us, but social imagination, moral imagination — these our technological slaves will never develop — these we ourselves have to develop.

Of the many things and phenomena that a child of pre-school age can know and really respond to without being intellectually stressed and burdened too early, I want to list a small selection: The seasons; the phases of the moon; the weather and precipitation; two to four constellations (Orion, the Great Bear). All the fruit and vegetables from the market; the different types of grain and what they are used for; a few woodland and park trees, ornamental bushes and flowers — provided the parents know them! The most important and dangerous poisonous plants. (Only a single class 2 boy recognized the deadly nightshade on a school-outing and prevented his fellow pupils from consuming the supposed blue-berries; the teacher knew it only by name.) A few breeds of dog, and all the birds that come to the bird-table. (True, a family living on the thirteenth floor of a high-rise block in the city *occasionally* see a pigeon at the window but apart from that, they assured me, they see no other animals in the wild state, year in, year out.) The names of all the objects and activities that the child sees in the house and in the neighbourhood. Parents should describe and explain them, using the correct terms. If there are workmen in the house, this provides a chance to learn the names of tools and to watch how different things are done. A lot can be learnt through watching. If building is going on in the neighbourhood the child can watch its progress and learn to recognize and name machines and the different working processes — provided that someone shows and explains them to him.

The child needs time, repetition, and additional explanations in order to cope with what has been learnt and experienced. If one is too lazy, too tired, too busy or distracted to answer one's children's questions thoroughly and in such a way that they are really told what they want to know and need for their understanding, then one leads them away from any desire to learn, and brings them up to be indifferent. Then no 'educational toy' will help, however expensive.

Education is transmitted by the illustrated book, unfortunately not by all. Before giving a child a book, one should check that everything is correct; children examine each illustration in detail and are annoyed by a carelessly illustrated book. A teacher gave as an example in a lecture a reader for beginners. One illustration showed the bars of a cage; a monkey hangs from above, but one does not see what he is hanging from; in front of the cage stands a child and holds a banana in the air. The text says: 'Where is the monkey? The monkey sits in the tree! Here, a nut! Come and eat, monkey!' Such a book should go into the fire and not into the hands of children. The child's ability to combine ideas is impaired by carelessly put together books. It does not matter if the illustrations are only faint indications or extremely stylized — they must correspond to the text! Just as illustrated books help to make the world comprehensible they should also awaken trust. Even where phantastical things are presented the book must not contradict itself, least of all through negligence.

Of quite a different nature is the 'upside-down world', where ideas are purposely interchanged: I take the room and sweep the brush! The mind is sharpened by this. At a certain age, rarely before the age of six, children can find this excruciatingly funny and like to try it for themselves. Shoes and socks are put on the hands, legs are slipped into sleeves, arms into trousers, and a cheeky face grins at one out of the fly. How sad that Mother is in a hurry to go to work and dismisses the joke as nonsense!

Now I want to list a number of the things which a child can already do by itself — and should be able to do — before starting school. Especially important: tying bows, for example on shoelaces. The method by which a two-year-old I know learnt is as follows: first, a simple knot is made; then part of *both* the laces is doubled and a simple knot again tied. As long as enough 'ends' have been left over, this makes a bow. At the age of three a child can dress and undress on its own and rarely needs help. This can even become a favourite game: a girl of three-and-a-half was visiting relatives; her mother had packed her clothes: two pairs of long trousers, three or four jumpers, underwear and perhaps even a dress. Although there were beautiful toys at her aunt's, they could provide no competition against the enormous fun of trying on endless variations of these clothes. In continuously changing combinations, they provided stimulation and activity for many days. Even after returning home, packing clothes, going off on her travels and changing remained the favourite game for quite some time. Fortunately no one complained that clothes were not for playing. Why not? Perhaps someone who was never allowed to play with clothes later has the greatest difficulty in dressing in such a way that she is also nice to look at. At an early stage a child can learn to fold its own clothes properly, and perhaps even small pieces of laundry.

Laying and clearing the table, washing and drying up, are a matter of course. Many a five-year-old can even prepare a simple meal.

Mother does the sewing. (Every child has certainly at some time tried snipping with scissors — into new material or its own clothes. There are plastic scissors which really cut only paper, but it is advisable to try them before buying, as some do not even cut paper and are completely useless.) Then embroidering pictures on to cardboard can be learnt. A four-year-old took great pains to sew and embroider a napkin-bag for his much-loved grandmother, and she has preserved and used it now for twenty years.

Sewing on buttons (even with the proper 'stalk') is great fun, and if it is on Father's pyjamas, also a great honour. However, Father then also has to be pleased in the evening and find appreciative words, otherwise he destroys the child's joy in creating. Praise, appreciation and participation in its joy are the crowning of all the child's efforts and achievements. If one indifferently denies it these, or even just blames it, orders it about and criticizes it all the time, one does not really love one's child and hinders the development of both its physical and mental faculties — even if one is otherwise all for intellectual advancement.

74

Children *have* to learn how to behave in traffic before starting school in order to stay alive. Turning left and right can be practised in the backyard with a scooter or a tricycle. The right — that is where he has the small mole or the thumb which he sucks — some kind of mark can be found on every child's hand. How to behave at traffic lights — one has to be careful: the child may be colour-blind. So red is on top, green at the bottom.

*

It is good if children learn in good time not only to notice faults but also to rectify them. The wooden paving in the courtyard of the kindergarten became dangerous because individual blocks rose up, thus causing people to trip. The old-age pensioner who trims the hedges and does odd-jobs out of the kindness of his heart and because he loves children would eventually have got round to doing something about them. But no — he does not need to bother: a group of children dig up the offending blocks, deepen their sand foundations with small trowels and replace them again all level. Since then a conscientious four-year-old checks the paving daily.

A few weeks later two children demolished a stool. With strong glue and a vice the damage was repaired. However, the two did not want to let any of the other children help them. To repair something they have damaged is of high educational value to children, gives great pleasure to the little 'vandals', and increases their self-confidence.

Up to the age of six a boy (who later became an economist) broke and spoilt all the good toys with which his brothers and sisters had already played. The broken pieces were kept at the time, and at the age of six he began to repair each piece with care and growing skill.

With plastic toys this would not have been possible. Once broken they can no longer be saved and must be thrown away. Unfortunately, many children receive this kind of toy, which can only be broken as a variation on playing with them; which in any case hardly stand up to normal usage, break, and are then thrown away. Such toys encourage callousness, which can later have its repercussions in the social sphere.

*

Children also have to learn to occupy themselves in their free time. Some can do this naturally and can think of more things to do than they can ever manage. The others have to learn it. One has to stimulate them, teach them skills. Otherwise in the holidays there come the well-known maternal groans: 'If only school would start again! This lot are really getting on my nerves'.

The shorter working week brings with it increasingly more leisure time. Where no interests and abilities have been developed, what remains to be done but illicit work or the passive killing of the time that has been so laboriously striven for? Teaching children to read as early as possible does not help in the least. Nor does it help in a job, for there it is important that one has learned and practised many things so that one can also rapidly acquire the specialist knowledge needed for the job.

Neither is the television screen an educational instrument for the small child. The television conveys information. An adult can critically assimilate this; older school children should also be able to do so. For a small child factual information is useless. It can be learnt by heart like 'hickory, dickory dock . . .', but does not mean anything.

Just how meaningless a piece of information can be was demonstrated by a little girl who had a baby brother when she was three-and-a-half. After a difficult birth, the mother had to stay in hospital for a long time and could only wave to her little daughter through a window. Finally mother and baby came home. 'Tomorrow I shall tell everyone in kindergarten that I have a baby brother', the little girl announced. — 'But did you not tell them before?' 'No, I didn't know it.' — 'But we told you about it every day!' 'You might have told me about it, but I didn't *know* it.' There we have it. A child does not want to be informed, it wants to experience. It wants to touch, have another look, ask. All this is impossible in front of the television. One can never say: 'Stop, we want to stay a bit longer with that big animal!' or 'We want to stroke that lamb.' Not even the favourite, 'Do it again!' is of any help. Any reaction of the child, any active participation in what is offered, is suppressed, crushed by the on-running programme and is 'trained *out*' of him.

Absolute passivity, the ideal consumer attitude, is bred. A film in the cinema, however, is preferable. One watches it oneself first and then prepares the children for it. Then one can go to see it two or three times and so let it become a real experience. Never will our eldest child forget *The Wonders of the Prairie*. With his brother it was Grzimek's *Serengeti*, which was the start of an episode of rhinoceros, antelope and zebra drawings.

Older school-children can assimilate information. It is nevertheless sad that magnificent ventures like Heyerdahl's *Ra* or Jacques Cousteau's explorations of the sea are shown late at night, whereas at a time when children can watch, banal serials are provided for their admiration.

The headmaster of a school in Völklingen was able to observe the shocking effect that television has on the learning ability of children. When the Saarland joined the federal German economic sphere in 1959, there was a considerable backlog of demand for electrical goods. Previously, very few people owned a television set. The headmaster was away from school at the time for several weeks because of heart trouble. After he had been teaching his Class 7 again for a few days, he asked nine children to stand up and asked them if they had meanwhile acquired a television set. Eight children confirmed this and the ninth said: 'We don't have one, but my grandmother has.' In this short time, the damage to the children's learning ability had become noticeable.

Not only the learning ability of the children, but their whole attitude to reality is influenced by television. Television children do not let themselves be impressed very easily — they know 'everything' from the television. Do they really know it? Or are they deluded into believing that they do?

Television approaches us with the claim that it gives an account of reality. The adults, who knows reality, knows how to judge this. But a child — ? For the child, the television becomes a false witness:

The cartoon cat is flattened, but soon rises again to cause new mischief.

A cowboy throws his arms into the air and falls off his horse.

A Vietnamese peasant's hut is blown into the air. Change of scene. Compassion?

A world famous orchestra gives a concert. A highly respected academic discusses a contemporary problem. Switch over! The thriller series is starting on the other channel! Respect?

As flitting shadows, murderer and victim, a football star, the Pope, monsters, President Carter appear. At the push of a button one disappears as fast as the other. How, then, is a sense for the individuality, the real being of another person supposed to develop in the inexperienced child?

Dolls and the Self

While conquering each sphere of his environment from game to game, assimilating and familiarizing himself with it, the child's own faculties develop from game to game in the most delicate and diverse of ways. Its senses become sharpened, it learns to control the instrument of its body, and gains the ability in a great variety of ways to relate to precisely that environment it has come to know through play. This is development in the true sense of that fine word: something until then unformed begins to shape itself so that it may come closer to the image which is its first beginning and its final aim. 'So God created man in his own image'.

All the games we have discussed so far affect the innermost sphere, the very being of the child, but there is one other game that properly belongs to this sphere: playing with dolls. *Through the doll the child finds its own self.* But the doll in its turn has such a strong effect on the child that it is not at all unimportant what our children's dolls consist of.

The eminent educator, Rudolf Steiner, founder of the Waldorf School Movement and homes for handicapped children, writes in his book, *The Education of the Child*[2]:

> As the muscles of the hand grow firm and strong in performing the work for which they are fitted, so the brain and other organs of the physical body of man are guided into the right lines of development if they receive the right impression from their environment. An example will best illustrate this point. You can make a doll for a child by folding up an old napkin, making two corners into legs, the other two corners into arms,

79

a knot for the head, and painting eyes, nose and mouth with blots of ink. Or else you can buy the child what they call a 'pretty' doll, with real hair and painted cheeks. We need not dwell on the fact that the 'pretty' doll is of course hideous, and apt to spoil the healthy aesthetic sense for a lifetime. The main educational question is a different one. If the child has before him the folded napkin he has to fill in from his own imagination all that is needed to make it real and human. This work of the imagination moulds and builds the forms of the brain. The brain unfolds as the muscles of the hand unfold when they do the work for which they are fitted. Give the child the so-called 'pretty' doll, and the brain has nothing more to do. Instead of unfolding, it becomes stunted and dried up. If people could look into the brain as the spiritual investigator can, and see how it builds its forms, they would assuredly give their children only such toys as are fitted to stimulate and vivify its formative activity. Toys with dead mathematical forms alone leave a desolating and killing effect upon the child. On the other hand everything that kindles the imagination works in the right way.

In these important comments, Rudolf Steiner gave only an indication of the imaginative powers of the small child. They are capable of amazing things!

When it was still normal to wrap new-born babies in swaddling clothes, one could buy a type of cloth that was pink on one side and blue on the other. Into such a pink-blue cloth the mother of a twenty-two month old boy bound a ball of darning wool to make a pink head; the blue tip of the cloth was laid over this head like a hood and the rest of the cloth folded up to the 'neck' and — blue side to the outside — firmly rolled up. Thus it became the semblance of a baby doll, and was given some durability by a ribbon bound crosswise round it. For about a year, this somewhat vague being was the child's first doll. It even had a name: the little boy called his doll 'Willy' after an infant from his parents' circle of friends, whose birth was announced just at that time. Willy could sleep, wake up, laugh and cry.

'Look! Willy's just waking up; he's opened one eye already!'

'Look! Willy's waving to you with his little hand!'

When Willy became dirty, Mother would unwrap him and then recreate the doll from a new cloth in front of the child. This dying and coming alive again, this 'reincarnation', in no way surprised the child and it also never occurred to him that his Willy lacked arms, legs, eyes, ears, nose and mouth. Nothing was missing; he had everything. Such is the power of a child's imagination.

When the boy was about three years old, Willy was replaced by the more distinctly formal 'Eckersly', with a carved wooden head. He was all-important for another two years; then he lay around unused for several years, until at the age of eleven the boy discovered him again and readopted him.

Great confidence in the power of the child's imagination is revealed in the moving scene from Paul Gallico's book, *Love of Seven Dolls*[14], where the little girl, Mouche, takes leave of the seven dolls she loves so much, and each one gives her a parting present. When it is the turn of the doll 'Monsieur Nicholas', who repairs and makes toys, and who also knows something about wounded human feelings, the story says:

. . . and Monsieur Nicholas gave her an oddly turned piece of wood that was not one but many shapes.

'For your first-born,' he said. 'It is a toy I have made for him that is not any, yet is still all toys, for in his imagination, when he plays with it, it will be whatever he sees in it, or wishes it to be.'

But in this most imaginative stage of childhood, not only does the piece of wood turn into a doll, but the doll can inadvertently turn into a block of wood. A two-year-old boy used to borrow the wooden doll, 'Tis', from an old fellow lodger. He loved Tis from the depths of his heart and treated him with great care. One day the cleaner came into the child's room and threw two briquettes into the stove. Hardly had the woman left the child when he threw the doll into the stove, the dearly loved doll, which at that moment had turned into a briquette. The child had no idea that the doll was in the stove and said quite confidently: 'Tis will come back.'

The age at which actual play with dolls starts varies, but it is round about the second year. This is the game that touches the depths of the personality; it not only educates, forms or misforms, like all other games, but here the child meets itself.

One may think that, essentially, playing with dolls is simply a game in which children imitate the way in which parents deal with their children. This may be partly true. Indeed, the game of many little girls with dolls is mainly a mother-and-child game, albeit a very serious one.

The following incident occurred during the Napoleonic Wars, and is described by Wilhelm von Kügelgen[9]:

> As there was no chair for the guest, Beckedorff removed the doll, Sally, which was buried under piles of scarves and shawls, from a still vacant chair and moved it to the table.
>
> At that moment my sister came running from some distant corner and buried her head in Mother's lap, screaming terribly. The whole company was startled; everybody jumped up and crowded round to look at the injury. They thought the child had hurt herself, perhaps knocked an eye out, and it took a long time until Mother succeeded in raising the head of the frantically crying girl to have a look, and in persuading her to speak. Finally, amid sobbing and coughing, the following calamity was revealed: the doll, Sally, extremely ill with scarlet fever, had been sweating it out, and whilst the poor mother who had no one to send to the chemist had had to go herself, Beckedorff had dragged the poor creature, so dangerously ill, from under her blankets and had put her on the cold window-sill, wearing only a nighty.

'And now', ended the desperate mother, and nearly choked at this sentence — 'and now Sally has surely caught cold!' So serious was the scene that no one laughed. On the contrary, everyone was concerned to comfort her and offer good advice as to how the chill could be rendered harmless. Let it be here observed that the doll suffered no further ill effects. The favourite doll — it can also be a teddy bear or some other small animal — is endowed with a bit of the child's own soul. The child feels that the doll's life stems from its own. I have known the following: a four-year-old possessed a doll which he had had from the age of two and called simply 'Dolly', and which was dressed like the boy himself. Once he was staying in a hotel in the Black Forest with his parents. In the evening the boy was given his meal early and put to bed, where he remained alone with his doll while his parents shared in the evening meal downstairs. At this point the child gave the doll a name: his own. Through this doubling of himself, testified by his giving the doll his own name, he hoped to hold his own better against loneliness and the strange surroundings. This doll, moreover, accompanied the boy for many more years. When he started reading James Fenimore Cooper, the doll was dressed up as an Indian. It had a soap-box on a roller-skate, underwent shipwreck in a stream one time, and even had a big parachute with which it made magnificent jumps — well strapped in and with crash-helmet — from the top storey of the house.

That not *more* boys — say from the age of two to six — have dolls, stems from the fact that we adults are shy of giving them to them. As if later only mothers had children, but fathers had shaggy bears!

And generally there are several distinctions made in the up-bringing of boys and girls that lack any justification. Why, for example, should a boy be less suited than a girl to looking after a smaller brother or sister? Why should only girls learn the niceties of housework? Yet more boys than girls join cooking courses for children. 'A boy does not cry!' What is that supposed to mean? Education to be tough and courageous? — But a woman needs courage more than a man if she wants to hold her own in this world. And toughness? A lot of things might be better if men's hearts were not so tough. And if we disregard the doll as a means of practising dealing with children, the doll as a second 'I' — as the being the child clasps in his arms when he is beyond himself in order to come to himself again — this can be just as necessary for a boy as for a girl.

It is only that boys' games with dolls rarely turn into the mother-and-child games of the girls. For this reason a boy's doll needs much less clothing than a girl's. A girl's doll is continually being dressed and undressed. A boy's doll can have its clothes sewn on, and if it needs new ones, they possibly have to look exactly the same as the previous ones. A seven-year-old let me dress his doll in new clothes, for after five years the old ones were falling off its rather sagging body. The doll was actually used only at night, but it had to be dressed exactly as before. A boy's doll, at most, occasionally needs a special outfit, but never a 'wardrobe'.

A boy of four or five years owned a 'Babutz', a bear made of bright-flowered material. Every day the boy played with a girl one year younger than himself. Occasionally Babutz was allowed to spend the night with the girl. The girl was a capricious creature, and well aware of her power over her faithful friend. So she said: 'I don't want Babutz today', whereupon the boy simply threw Babutz over the high fence into the girl's garden. Then he was finally taken into the house: he was after all some*one* and not just some*thing*. Is this not similar to a lover's later laying or offering part of his own being at the feet of his love? Not imitation — but anticipation.

A nurse had already cared for many infants and older children when she was given the task of winning back to life a five-year-old girl who had nearly died of a serious illness and just could not recover. With tiny portions of vegetarian food the child was slowly weaned back to eating again. All the love and experience of the nurse were required to rouse the *joie de vivre* of childhood. Then a setback occurred: a beloved uncle, who used to visit the house frequently, suddenly died. A few days later the child came to the nurse with her favourite doll — it was called Liselotte after the child's mother — and announced sadly that it had died. The nurse tried to dissuade the child from thinking this, but the fact remained that the doll was dead. A beautiful box was chosen as a coffin and the doll was ceremoniously buried in a quiet corner. 'Now she is dead', the girl said at last, 'and perhaps she will never return; or perhaps only when we are very old.' Then the child was silent and the nurse as well. — After about ten minutes the child came running excitedly to the nurse and said: 'Listen, she called!' Then both were very relieved; the child hurried to open the grave and the coffin, and clasped the resurrected doll in her arms with great caressing. Through this, that part of the child's soul which was 'chrysalized' in the doll had overcome death, and the health of the little girl began to improve. To such lengths can play with dolls go!

Since, therefore, a doll can be of such importance to a child, adults should be just as conscious and careful in their treatment of the doll as they are in their treatment of the child. The mother must know the dolls; she must know in which ones a part of her child's soul is living. For this can change with circumstances! One doll can take the place of a previous one, and quite a bit of tact is necessary on the part of adults if they do not want to be continually making a *faux pas*.

How, as children, we used to despise those people who ventured to deride our wooden dolls! What is really happening, and where does it lead, if a child remains faithful to an unattractive favourite doll which is ridiculed by everyone else? Out of faithfulness to such a wretched, despised creature, out of this faithfulness, can grow the strength which later enables a mother to stand by the child to which nature has been unkind, her feeble-minded or deformed child, of which she can never be proud, and to bestow on him her special love.

One has to be careful: the oldest and most decrepit doll can play an important and mysterious role in a child's life. One does well to treat such a scarecrow, loved to shreds, with respect; one can patch, clean and repair the unsightly, tattered doll, even put new parts on it, but under no circumstances may one throw it away as long as it 'lives'. Otherwise one harms the child and deprives oneself of part of the child's trust.

A girl, born during the war, played with a rag doll which had been sewn together by her mother. From time to time the mother washed the thing in the tub and hung it up on the line to dry. Such a doll survives this kind of treatment without harm. Then the mother became seriously ill. She had to go into hospital and the child and the doll were accommodated with a childless aunt — the child with love and care, but the doll was burned in the stove as 'revolting and absolutely rotten' . . . The child never again attached itself to a doll, never again risked part of her own being in a doll. I know parents whose first child died young, and who never found the courage to have another. Something similar probably happened in this little girl. This story lies twenty years in the past. It has not been forgiven.

Such tragedies happen where the adult takes the doll to be simply a 'thing'. The child experiences with horror and dismay the cruelty of the adult to the 'living' doll; the adult, on the other hand, is surprised at the 'hysterical fuss' of the child about a piece of old rubbish. The adult who destroys a doll, an 'active' doll, in the belief that it is only a 'thing', is in approximately the same position as the unfortunate lorry driver who let his lorry run over an old cardboard box lying in the road — but it was a box in which a little child had hidden itself . . .

Maria Melchers also describes a violent parting with a doll[15]:

'Where is my Tulla?' Father ignores the question. 'Didn't you bring Tulla?' Now Father has to admit: 'I couldn't. Mummy burnt her.' Burnt — ? Tulla! Burnt — ?' The stare of the child expresses disbelief, horror and a nameless grief. 'No, Daddy, say you're joking. Quickly, say you're joking and give her to me.'

The father finds it infinitely difficult to extinguish the last faint ray of hope.

'Maria, child', he says as gently and affectionately as only Father can express it, 'you must be reasonable and understand Mummy. You are a big girl now, and Tulla was meant to be a little girl's toy, and it was time it was burnt.'

Maria stands thunderstruck. She does not cry or complain. Silently she looks down in front of her. After a while she says in a quiet voice:

'Tulla, — that was part of me. — Tulla, that is — '

She is silent; she wanted to say: 'My childhood', but she does not say it out loud; she only thinks it, and has the feeling that a gate has closed, a golden gate, which can never, never again open.

Now one might argue that the world would be filled with wrecks of dolls that are not allowed to be thrown away! Not at all: the doll is rather like the chrysalis of the butterfly*. When the chrysalis has hatched, then only the empty wrapping is left for which there is no further use. That part

* In German the words for 'doll' and 'chrysalis' are the same: *Puppe*. There is a similar connection in English between 'puppet' and 'pupa'.

of the child which is 'chrysalized' in its favourite doll also one day frees itself, and the child itself will deal with the empty shell. It may say: 'Let's put my old doll away in the loft now', or 'let's give it away.' One can easily wait till then. I do not know of a single case of a child who played with dolls up to its fifteenth year and even beyond coming to any harm through it.

The wish for a doll should be granted. Not having a doll when it needs one can make life more difficult for a child. Annie Hamilton Donell writes of such a case in her novel about childhood, *Rebecca Mary*[16].

The kind-hearted minister's wife has beautifully dressed a friendly-looking doll for the lonely little Rebecca Mary, and hands the doll over to strict Aunt Olivia, with whom the child lives. The present is received in chilly silence.

'For Rebecca Mary,' the minister's wife was saying, in a rather halting way. 'I dressed it for her. I thought perhaps she never —'

'She never', said Aunt Olivia, briefly. Strange that at that particular instant she should remember a trifling incident in the child's far-off childhood. The incident had to do with a little white night-gown rolled tightly and pinned together. She had found Rebecca Mary in her little waist and petticoat cuddling it in bed.

'It's a dollie. Please '*sh*, Aunt Olivia, or you'll wake her up!' the child had whispered, in an agony. 'Oh, you're going to turn her back to a night-gown? Don't unpin her, Aunt Olivia — it will kill her! I'll name her after you if you'll let her stay.'

'Get up and take your clothes off.' Strange Aunt Olivia should remember at this particular instant; should remember, too, that the pin had been a little rusty and came out hard. Rebecca Mary had slid out of bed obediently, but there had been a look on her little brown face as of one bereaved. She had watched the pin come out and the night-gown unroll, in stricken silence. When it hung released and limp over Aunt Olivia's arm she had given one little cry:

'She's dead!'

The Aunt feels it her duty not to give the new doll to the child either. The minister's wife tries to discover whether this happened or not.

'Come in, Rebecca Mary,' the minister's wife said, cordially. 'Don't you want to see the new dress Rhoda's doll is going to have? I suppose you could make your doll's dress yourself?' It seemed a hard thing to say. Feeling round was not pleasant.

'P'haps I could, but she doesn't wear dresses,' Rebecca Mary answered, gravely.

'No?' This was puzzling. 'Her clothes don't come off, I suppose?' Then it could not be the nice, friendly doll.

'No'm. Nor they don't go on either. She isn't a feel doll.'

'A — what kind did you say, dear?' The minister's wife paused in her work interestedly. Distinctly, Miss Olivia had not given her *the* doll; but this doll — 'I don't think I quite understood, Rebecca Mary.'

'No'm; its a little hard. She isn't a *feel* doll, I said. I never had a feel one. Mine hasn't any body, just a soul. But she's a great comfort.'

'Robert,' appealed the minister's wife, helplessly. This was a case for the minister — a case of souls.

'Tell us some more about her' Rebecca Mary,' the minister urged, gently. But there was helplessness, too, in his eyes.

'Why, that's all!' returned Rebecca Mary in surprise. 'Of course I can't dress her or undress her or take her out calling. But its a great comfort to rock her soul to sleep.'

'Call Rhoda,' murmured the minister's wife to the minister; but Rhoda was already there. She volunteered prompt explanation. There was no hesitation in Rhoda's face.

'She means a make-believe doll. Don't you Rebecca Mary?'

'Yes,' Rebecca Mary assented; 'that's her other name, I suppose, but I never called her by it.'

'What did you call her?' demanded practical Rhoda. 'What's her name, I mean?'

'Rhoda!' — hastily, from the minister's wife. This seemed like sacrilege. But Rhoda's clear, blue eyes were fixed upon Rebecca Mary; she had not heard her mother's warning little word.

A shy color spread thinly over the lean little face of Rebecca

Mary. For the space of a breath or two she hesitated. 'Her name's — Felicia,' then, softly.

That is the name of the deeply affected minister's wife. Later the Aunt surprises the child as it is rocking its empty arms and quietly singing:

Oh, hush, oh, hush, my dollie;
Don't worry anymore,
For Rebecca Mary 'n' the angels
Are watching o'er,
— O'er 'n' o'er 'n' o'er.

Only then does the child receive the doll given by the minister's wife, and that homeless part of the child's soul can finally be fostered in a visible house.

Here a borderline case is described. No invisible doll would have come into being if a visible, a 'feel' doll, had been available in time — even had it been only the rolled up nighty.

It is a different case with invisible playmates. It is by no means rare that children surround themselves with invisible companions. Of three sisters, born in successive springs, the middle one acquired an invisible companion at the start of her third year. Suddenly 'Galle' appeared and was taken seriously straight away by the whole family. Shortly after driving off, the father stopped the car again and opened the door because 'Galle' had forgotten to get in in time. Fortunately 'Galle' got her own car a few days later. Most of the time, 'Galle' was about the size of a child, but she could make herself so small that she could slip through a key-hole. She was also sometimes visible and sometimes invisible.

Just at that time the little girl was going through a difficult developmental stage accompanied by many terrible tantrums. When the family moved to America, 'Galle' was not mentioned on the ship. But, over there, she straight away appeared again. Then the oldest sister also adopted a 'Galle', perhaps out of jealousy. This 'Galle' was more or less an imitation of the original one and received little attention. The original 'Galle', however, acquired a following of 'Gille', 'Pumpum', 'Sasa' and 'Nädldä'. These four beings appeared only in the company of 'Galle', whereas she herself was quite capable of undertaking things on her own. On walks 'Galle' sometimes went ahead, or she ran crying along behind. At table she was occasionally reminded to put her elbows down. 'Galle' slept very lightly; when she was asleep, the family had to walk on tiptoes. She belonged to it completely — for over a year.

When the family left America after a year and returned to Germany, 'Galle' was not mentioned again. Later the mother learned that 'Galle', 'Gille', 'Pumpum', 'Sasa' and 'Nädldä' had all drowned together on the crossing. From that point on, the tantrums of the child grew rarer and less severe.

Whereas the older and the younger sisters were loving dolls' mothers, dolls never really came alive for this child, although she certainly played with them, too.

Another small girl, who only had a brother five years older, looked after at least three invisible little sisters for a long time. They were called 'Gisele-Roggele-Bag', 'Gisele-Stetten' and 'Halbele'; sometimes there were even more of them! One after the other, the little invisible ones were lifted on to the swing and pushed, while the others were reminded to sit nice and quietly on the grass and not to run under the swing. Before the child went to school, however, her little sisters disappeared and the girl confided in me: 'Now I'm playing with bigger children.' These, too, had names. This child often played alone, and was never bored.

In its invisible playmates the child experiences, for a time, a part of its own being as an independent person — sometimes as a 'conscience' and adviser, in other cases as a kind of scapegoat. This might have been the case with the 'Hunters' who, a father told me, his daughter alleged to have done all kinds of naughty things. Or the child has lost something, and now allots what is lost to its invisible companions — and thus again to itself.

The disappearance of an invisible companion, the discarding of a doll, are important steps on the path of the child to itself. Being able to do without these supports, it becomes independent. — If, however, one removes them forcibly and before the child is ready, then one makes it unsure of itself.

A doll can have an accident. It can get lost on a walk in the woods, or is put down in a nice place in the park and forgotten. With a shock one returns: it is gone. Even an advertisement in the paper does not bring it back. The pain is unbearable. After the war I read of a mother whose child had slipped out of its swaddling clothes on her arm as she fled, and had got lost. None of the other terrible refugee stories so shook me with compassion. In the same way I lost my 'Haldagele' out of its swaddling clothes in my grandmother's garden and mourned its death. Sorrow, pain, pangs of conscience and the feeling of one's own guilt. Many a night did I cry myself to sleep. My father had carved 'Haldagele' out of the pale wood of the lime tree and it was no consolation to find it a few months later, black and mouldy, among a pile of leaves. It was never the same again, although it still exists today, scrubbed to a fairly light grey colour.

What can one do in the face of such misery? One must try to comfort the child, help to foster the idea that another child has found the lost loved one and taken it in. Sometimes a substitute can be found: something as much the same as possible — or something completely new. Perhaps even something living. One should *not* say that it was just a doll. Of course it was a doll — but then, what is a doll?

The roles a doll has to play, according to the circumstances, are of such a complex and varied nature that one can readily understand that the more indistinct and undefined its expression the less trouble it will cause the imagination of the child. One need only think of the expressions of certain dolls which neither cry nor laugh, and can therefore be believed capable of doing both.

If a doll has a clearly defined character, then this is certainly respected, and made use of in play — though it is mostly assigned to a specific role. As a second 'I' it is less useful, even if it is often used as such for lack of anything better.

Puppets, on the other hand, are meant to personify a well-defined trait of character. Here the many aspects of human nature are divided between individual dolls, each with a strictly laid down character. In reply to Mouche's question to the puppets (Gallico[14]): 'But who are you then, Monsieur Nicholas? Who are you all?' he spoke:

'A man is many things, Mouche. He may wish like Carrot Top to be a poet and soar to the stars and yet be earthbound and overgrown, ugly and stupid like Alifanfaron. In him will be the seeds of jealousy, greed and the insatiable appetite for admiration and pleasure of chicken-brained arrogant Gigi. Part of him will be a pompous bore like Dr Duclos and another the counterpart of Madame Muscat, gossip, busybody, tattletale and sage. And where there is a philosopher there can also be sly, double-dealing sanctimonious hypocrite, thief and self-forgiving scoundrel like Mr Reynardo.'

And Monsieur Nicholas continued: 'The nature of man is a never-ending mystery, Mouche. There we are, Mouche, seven of us you have grown to love. And each of us has given you what there was of his or her heart. I think I even heard the wicked Reynardo offer to lay down his life for you — or his skin. He was trying to convey to you a message from Him who animates us all . . .'

93

Only the whole 'Punch-and-Judy family' taken together makes a complete human being. Charles Dickens, in chapter 16 of *The Old Curiosity Shop*, mentions the main Punch-and-Judy characters:

> Perhaps his [Punch's] imperturbable character was never more strikingly developed, for he preserved his usual equable smile notwithstanding that his body was dangling in a most uncomfortable position, all loose and limp and shapeless, while his long peaked cap, unequally balanced against his exceedingly slight legs, threatened every instant to bring him toppling down. . . . The hero's wife and one child, the hobby-horse, the doctor, the foreign gentleman who not being familiar with the language is unable in the representation to express his ideas otherwise than by the utterance of the word 'Shallabalah' three distinct times, the radical neighbour who will by no means admit that a tin bell is an organ, the executioner, and the Devil, were all here.

But what happens in reality when real caricature enters the nursery? Where does it lead if distorted pictures are shown before the real image is even known, and long before the child has acquired any standards whereby it can recognize the distortion as such? Contact with caricatures can harm the child.

In the following extract[17], H. H. Schöffler quotes the most convincing example of the harmful effects of caricature on small children as described by the Professor of Child Therapy, Alfred Nitschke:

> Thus the fact that Rudolf Steiner gave priority to the two fundamental phenomena, 'the infant lives totally in imitation' and 'the whole infant is a sense organ' should never be forgotten. To what extent this extremely exposed position of the infant as sense organ admits the environment, emerges with shattering clarity from a . . . casuistical example by Alfred Nitschke:
> 'A ten-month-old girl, with a long history of illness (lack of appetite, frequent 'unmotivated' vomiting) was admitted to

hospital. No physical symptoms of illness could be diagnosed, but the child was wretchedly thin, her muscular system weak and flaccid. She could not sit. Most of the time she assumed a peculiar position: the body rested between the outstretched legs like a closed penknife. In addition, her limp arms often lay stretched forward on the cover. Her resting face was raised a little, her ill-humoured and listless expression indicating rejection. Particularly noticeable, too, was her still, wide gaze, and even more a very expressive mouth with which the child often played with her fingers.

'This description seemed to indicate clearly to us that, according to previous experience, the excessive insecurity of the mother had both triggered off and fostered the mischief. In such cases, too, anxiety and tension are transmitted to the infant by the manner of dealing with it, by every look and word. In the clinic, such a child soon finds its balance through the relaxed assurance of experienced nurses. But this time our expectations were confounded. During her next three months in the clinic nothing changed, despite intensive efforts. — In talks with the parents we searched for other causes of the disturbance, which we suspected might exist, but could discover nothing.

'On the day on which this child was to be shown in a lecture as one of those in relation to whom we had not managed to discover and overcome a problem which probably lay in her environment, she was allowed to take something familiar with her, so as not to be too unhappy. This was a big rabbit which the child had brought from home as her favourite companion, and which she had continuously had in bed with her. The sight of this animal suddenly brought inspiration: this is the cause of the trouble! We remembered now how we had jokingly said when the child was admitted: The child looks like her rabbit. It was a large animal, one of those grotesque shapes which today are given to children as toys, with very long, thin, limply hanging arms and legs, and a head with strikingly large, fixed eyes, and a pronounced mouth, whose lips the child was continually touching. This flaccid and ill-humoured looking rabbit the child had often placed on the bedcovers facing herself, and in exactly her own attitude: the torso between the limp hind legs, the front legs stretched out, the face with that strange expression of eyes and mouth turned towards her. At home, this was more or less the only partner of the child, otherwise isolated from the outside world. This was the image of posture, movement and mood with which the child had been associated, on which she had modelled herself.

'I should not dare to give this interpretation in such a decided manner if the results of the treatment had not turned out to be so successful. We replaced the rabbit by a friendly-looking lamb of nearly the same size, which stood upright and had a well-defined shape. The child soon grew attached to the new animal. Although we in no way changed the treatment, the child began to eat with enjoyment after a few days, soon developed a natural childish gaiety, sat up, and forgot her former posture without any help from us. — The change reached right into the depths of the little person. For us it was marvellous, almost shattering after the long fruitless struggle — for the mother incomprehensible. This happy development has not broken off since the girl went home.'

This clinical example shows with tragic clarity how readily and uncritically the infant absorbs the outside world and buries it in the depths of its metabolism. The whole outside world, whether it makes its influence through movement or image, thus proves to be a symbol of the impress it will make on the development of the body.

What seems funny to adults can harm the child. Let us therefore ban all these horrors made of plastic from the nursery, and let us *not* hang Walt Disney figures on the wall. Wallpaper with figures on it is also not suitable for the nursery. *One* really beautiful picture, one wall-hanging, offer the child more than the same silly cat-scene a hundred times over. Nor need one fear that children could be over-taxed by looking at a real work of art. They do not take more from it than they can cope with. 'Let that which is most beautiful be given to the eye first; spare the expectant soul of the child the misshapen and the dissonant,' said Jean Paul.

Spare it! This sometimes requires quite a lot of courage as well as tact, depending on who presents such a nursery-horror. If in doubt, the interests of the child come first. One keeps the monster back, and carefully makes the donor aware that next time a ball, for example, would be more appreciated — there is nothing to get spoiled in that. There are also selfless friends who leave the choice of presents to the parents, and send them money now and then for this purpose. From my childhood I can remember wonderful presents which were announced, according to the giver, as a 'Michael-surprise' or an 'Aunt-Julie-surprise', and which filled us with deep gratitude towards the distant donors.

The more one thinks about what dolls should be like, the sadder one becomes at the sight of what is usually offered in the toy departments of our stores. Even eyes that close are too mechanical — a little girl praised her doll with its wooden head: 'My Tommy does not always need to go to sleep straight away, he can also lie awake sometimes.'

Walk, talk, cry, laugh, eat, drink, wet itself, blush, get a temperature, get brown in the sun — *any rag-doll, any nice, simple doll can do that in the hands of a child.* The mechanical creatures on the toy market can do it much less well, and provoke every older or younger brother into opening them up to have a look — and rightly so! Because these are not dolls, but machines, whose mechanics leave no room for the little bit of the child's soul that seeks to enclose itself there.

I consider dolls that can cry and shed 'real' tears a perverse monstrosity. They teach sadism! Just imagine: a mother purposely does something to her child *so that it cries* to amuse her friends! A defenceless 'child' is made to cry for fun. This is more cruel than when the wicked witch in the fairy tale is pushed into the oven in which she wanted to roast Gretel.

In Clemen Brentano's fairy-tale of 'Gockel, Hinckel und Gackeleia' occurs the sentence:
'Keine Puppe, es ist nur
eine schöne Kunstfigur.
(It is no doll, but only a mechanical figure.)
And whoever is familiar with the story knows what disaster befell the child through the mechanical figure.

If, however, something is to be said about these horrors, these children's enemies, let us quote Harlacher[1] once more:

And now someone else stands at the door and demands entry into the children's room: 'Cindy' ('Barbie', 'Action-Man'). Demands? Has been in for a long time — in business — with yearly profits of nearly a billion dollars and advertising expenditure of twelve million. The Barbie-Club has 800,000 members in the U.S.A. alone. In Sweden, 471,000 dolls and 1,775,000 outfits for them were sold to 350,000 girls. This doll is not designed for children, but *for the business with children*. With her, the ignorance of the parents is exploited, and their indifference is grist for the mill of those who do not want to let children grow up and develop any further, but want to make money out of them before they have sufficient resistance and are 'fit' to face all the commercial tricks. It has been said that if there were a dolls' heaven and a dolls' hell, Barbie would go to hell.

From 'Barbie' and her commercially successful sisters it is only a small step to the big show-dolls, those life-size monsters with expensive outfits that walk, dance, speak, and goodness knows what else. It is the doll that each girl in the street takes out for walks, presents to her friends, lets them admire — even the price the children know. Ownership of such a doll can be the pre-condition for full acceptance into the children's section of an affluent society. At home, the expensive piece is carefully pushed aside in its chair or bed, and with relief the little girl plays with the dolls she loves.

Dictated by commercial interests, encouraged by our

thoughtless affluent society, the show-off doll is the first of life's deceits with which our children are burdened. One hears the objection: 'But the children want it.' Two things can be answered to this. First, it is possible that a child badly wants such a doll — though questionable whether because of the doll itself, or because of the prestige it confers among other children. Second, it often happens that children demand something that is bad for them. We do not give them everything they want to eat. However, just as there are children who know what foods are good for them, so there are others who reject unwholesome toys.

Where mothers are sure of their position, and do not let their own lives be governed by the prevailing opinions, the children will not be easily dazzled by tasteless toys. During a painful illness, a little girl had a doll made for her which she called with her own name. This girl abruptly refuses to accept any other doll given to her since then. Either she says: 'I don't want that doll', or, in full view of the disappointed donor, the expensive present is even thrown on the floor and trampled on. Mother then has to see how to conciliate her guest, without, however, trying to force the doll on the child after all.

The child should feel free. It should not suffer coercion — either through the parents or through society. It is a torment for a child if it is forced into an outsider position to which it is not equal. Not to belong is painful. Most children want to stand out as little as possible from their friends in clothing and hair style. Clothes that are too plain or old fashioned may certainly still seem good to the mother, but make her daughter — despite the 'excellent quality of the cloth' — into the Cinderella of the class. However exquisite an embroidered smock, the fact that it called forth the ridicule of the other boys in the school can belong to the most bitter of childhood memories.

On the other hand, the lad who is allowed to grow his hair long will not always want the laborious task of looking after his fine shoulder-length locks. He will come in his own time to have two or four inches trimmed off — if only for the sake of convenience. To the shocked: 'How can you allow that!' I take care to answer: 'As long as neither his morals nor his health suffer — why not?'

On occasions, a prestige toy can be the only way of preventing a sensitive child from becoming an outsider. Children differ. What is good for one can be harmful for another. Even among brothers and sisters, one can always want to fit in with the group, while another has enough self-confidence to swim against the stream as well sometimes.

For one of the first lessons after the Christmas holidays, the First Class children were allowed to bring their favourite Christmas present to school. One of the small girls proudly set out with a new weaving-loom. 'And what did the other children get?' Mother enquired at lunch time. 'O, Mummy, they got horrible stuff! Imagine, dolls which talk stupidly, and dolls which wet themselves — horrible!' 'But didn't anyone receive something nice? Wasn't there something you thought you would have liked to have, too?' The child thought hard about it — then, quite convinced: 'No, nothing!'

The refusal of the prestige toy — the pride of the nonconformist, likewise the reverse refusal to be friends with someone who does *not* possess such a toy — the pride of the conformist, reflect for the most part the attitudes of the home.

If the nonconformist does not pay any attention to public opinion then this should not immediately be misinterpreted as social failure. It was the very girl with the weaving-loom who had taken on the task of 'taming', by means of kindness and little gifts, the boy in her class who was rejected by all the rest and was the naughtiest and most aggressive of them all. She thought: 'He's bound to be bad if nobody likes him.' The mother played no part in this decision. Three years later the same girl again upset the conformists by becoming friends with the poorest boy among her schoolfellows — this time the son of an asocial father. At least this protégé was not aggressive. Conformists certainly have a simpler life. Above all, however, they are economically useful.

Antoine de Saint-Exupéry enlarges on the phenomenon in the 71st chapter of his book *Citadelle*[18]:

I have forbidden the merchants to extol their wares too much. Because they soon develop into schoolmasters and teach you something as aim, which is essentially only means, and when they have fooled you about the path you have to follow, they humiliate you soon after; for if their music is vulgar, they produce a vulgar soul for you and then they can dispose of their wares on you. Now it is good, without a doubt, that things were created to serve man; but it would go against nature if man were created to serve as dustbin for the things.

Primal Memories

While, in the mother's womb, the child's earthly body is built up, develops and struggles to get from its confinement into the wide world, its soul comes from the vastness of eternity into the confinement of the physical body. The memory of the glory and splendour of their pre-birth existence, which all children have initially, usually fades very quickly:

> Our birth is but a sleep and a forgetting:
> The soul that rises with us, our life's star,
>> Hath had elsewhere its setting,
>> And cometh from afar;
>> Not in entire forgetfulness,
>> And not in utter nakedness,
> But trailing clouds of glory do we come
>> From God, who is our home.
> Heaven lies about us in our infancy;
> Shades of the prison-house begin to close
>> Upon the growing boy,
> But he beholds the light, and whence it flows.
>> He sees it in his joy;
> The youth, who daily farther from the east
>> Must travel, still is Nature's priest,
>> And by the vision splendid
>> Is on his way attended;
> At length the man perceives it die away,
> And fade into the light of common day.*

Conscientious description of the clinging to, and wanting to speak about, these paradisal memories occur throughout the obviously autobiographical novel by Maria Melchers, *Kirchstrasse 22*[15]. Repeatedly, the author de-

* Wordsworth, *Ode: Intimations of Immortality.*

scribes two counter-running developments: as long as memory persists, the child lacks the means of expressing it; and with the growing ability to express itself, the child feels how what it wants to impart fades from its memory.

Maria's first memory is of standing at the top of a high flight of stairs, looking down into the depths. Maria knows she must not let go of the banister, or else that terrible thing will attack her . . . But stronger than that which yawns up at her from the abyss, incomprehensible and awful, is the other, the familiar, which draws her so pleasantly. She only needs to cup the palm of her free right hand and hold it up a little, to be filled with a feeling of weightlessness and the blissful knowledge that there was a time when no chasm could frighten her, when she floated through realms flooded with light, in her hand the great ball, and around her . . .

If only she could remember how it was — the unimaginable. When it was? Where?

Her head resting on the banister, Maria stands and listens deep within herself. Very softly the clouds are about to part, sweet shadowy figures to become visible — when the hand of her mother brings her back down to earth, shattering the vision.

Lovingly bending over her, the tall, beautiful woman chides her little daughter and is convinced that she understands. What she does not know is that her child still possesses the delicate wings that are able to remove her from her present existence to where the realm of the origin of all things glimmers behind veils woven out of innate yearning and fading dream-like memories, and that being suddenly, incomprehensibly wrenched back causes the painful crying which will not be quieted for a long time . . .

But the memory of standing at the border of these intermediate lands remains with the child a lifetime.

Occasionally the child tried to express something of what it once knew, for example at the visit of a neighbour whose newborn child had died:

. . . small children whom God has called back — ? That is all dark, incomprehensible. There are so many questions to ask, but that is not allowed. When grown-ups talk, one has to keep silent. But: — enough angels in heaven — that is a sentence which fires the soul. One has to say something, even if it is forbidden. . . . 'Frau Hamacher, it is beautiful in heaven — but there are not angels enough! More have to come — more and more — until all are there.' Mother says quietly: 'What does a child know of harsh reality!'

Later, when she is twelve, a well-loved aunt shows her a picture of a child and says:

'This is my dear little sister. When she died at the age of nine, she promised me she would come down from heaven and tell me how it is up there near God. She did not keep her word; she has forgotten me.'

Maria turns round and faces her aunt with a distant look in her darkly shining eyes and says slowly and solemnly: 'No, not forgotten; only it could not happen how you imagined it. This is not only your little sister. It is also me, and I was sent to tell you how it is near God. Only it took too long till I could tell you. You did not know what I wanted when I was small, and that is a pity because it is only when you are small and do not have the right words that you really know what it was like before. Later on you have to search and search and you only know that at one time it was glorious, and that one day it will become glorious again when the soul no longer wears its earthly dress, when it is free and people say you are dead. You see, I had to tell you all that, and I have always known it.

Not the direct memory of eternity, but the lustre which is shed over childhood through this being still at home in paradise is also described by Wordsworth in his Ode:

> There was a time when meadow, grove, and stream,
> The earth, and every common sight,
> To me did seem
> Apparelled in celestial light,
> The glory and the freshness of a dream.
> It is not now as it hath been of yore —
> Turn wheresoe'er I may,
> By night or day,
> The things which I have seen I now can see no more.

This primal memory is experienced and then slowly lost. It enlivens many an early game or even transfigures it.

The next archetypal experience however, the incarnation of the soul into the physical body, is the subject of countless games: every child loves to slip into tight containers, nooks and crannies, cupboards, barrels, chests, boxes and baskets — unfortunately also fridges, which has repeatedly led to fatal accidents. It is widely held that the child thus plays itself, as it were, in the confines and security of the womb. This seems to me to be true in only the rarest of cases; *this* state of mind would seem to be true rather when the child is in its mother's arms or on her lap. In the box, after all, it slides around, in the barrel it rolls. From my own early childhood I remember how I always tried to carry myself around in my mother's large shopping basket. Judging by the size of the basket, I must have been about two and a half years old, three at the most. In most cases the children are intent on making it homely in their tight compartments.

In the magazine *Erziehungskunst*[17], Gerda Scheer describes the following scene in the article on work in the kindergarten:

> In a corner of the room, a small house is just under construction. The big girls are working there. They tie a few pieces of coloured cloth to hooks and thus make a wall. Towards the window they spread several pieces of coloured cloth over a rack and lay them so carefully next to each other that not the smallest gap remains in this wall. A specially big cloth serves as a roof. — One can see the enthusiasm shining from the children's eyes, so snug and protected do they feel in their dusky cave as they take possession, like bright souls entering a small dark human body . . .

The children are playing at becoming incarnated.

Children at Play
Everywhere and at all Times

In earlier times no one thought of talking and writing so much about children's games as is the case today. Children just played. They were allowed to play. It is only in our civilized and technological age that a certain effort is unavoidable to make it possible for our children to play at all.

The mechanized world of our cities, organized down to the last detail, is the most unsuitable place for playing one can think of. Even the unattractive places on the outskirts of the cities — ruins, waste-land with bushes and unhygienic rubbish dumps — offer more possibilities for play than the playgrounds in the cities — naturally also more dangers.

Incomparably richer, and also more dangerous, are (or were!) the games of the children of some of the peoples that stand outside our civilization. The pure-blooded Sioux Indian, Dr Charles Eastman (Ohiyesa), describes the games of his boyhood in the early sixties of the last century, in the very interesting book *Indian Boyhood*[19]:

> The Indian boy was a prince of the wilderness. He had but very little work to do during the period of his boyhood. His principal occupation was the practice of a few simple arts in warfare and the chase. Aside from this, he was master of his time.
>
> Whatever was required of us boys was quickly performed:

then the field was clear for our games and plays. There was always keen competition among us. We felt very much as our fathers did in hunting and war — each one strove to excel all the others.

It is true that our savage life was a precarious one, and full of dreadful catastrophes; however, this never prevented us from enjoying our sports to the fullest extent. As we left our teepees in the morning, we were never sure that our scalps would not dangle from a pole in the afternoon! It was an uncertain life, to be sure. Yet we observed that the fawns skipped and played happily while the gray wolves might be peeping forth from behind the hills, ready to tear them limb from limb.

Our sports were molded by the life and customs of our people; indeed, we practiced only what we expected to do when grown. Our games were feats with the bow and arrow, foot and pony races, wrestling, swimming and imitation of the customs and habits of our fathers. We had sham fights with mud balls and willow wands; we played lacrosse, . . . shot winter arrows (which were used only in that season) . . .

A leading arrow was shot at random into the air. Before it fell to the ground a volley from the bows of the participants followed. Each player was quick to note the direction and speed of the leading arrow and he tried to send his own at the same speed and at equal height, so that when it fell it would be closer to the first than any of the others . . .

We had some quiet plays which we alternated with the more severe and warlike ones . . . In the winter we coasted much. We had no 'double-rippers' or toboggans, but six or seven of the long ribs of buffalo, fastened together at the large end, answered all practical purposes. Sometimes a strip of basswood bark, four feet long and about six inches wide, was used with considerable skill. We stood on one end and held the other, using the slippery inside of the bark for the outside, and thus coasting down long hills with remarkable speed.

The spinning of tops was one of the all-absorbing winter sports. We made our tops heart-shaped of wood, horn or bone. We whipped them with a long thong of buckskin. The handle was a stick about a foot long and sometimes we whittled the stick to make it spoon-shaped at one end.

We played games with these tops — two to fifty boys at one time. Each whips his top until it hums; then one takes the lead and the rest follow in a sort of obstacle race. The top must spin all the way through. There were bars of snow over which we must pilot our top in the spoon end of our whip; then again we would toss it in the air on to another open spot of ice or smooth snow-crust from twenty to fifty paces away. The top that holds out the longest is the winner.

Sometimes we played 'medicine dance'. This, to us, was almost what 'playing church' is among white children, but our people seemed to think it an act of irreverence to imitate these dances, therefore performances of this kind were always enjoyed in secret. We used to observe all the important ceremonies and it required something of an actor to reproduce the dramatic features of the dance. The real dances occupied a day and a night, and the program was long and varied, so that it was not easy to execute all the details perfectly; but the Indian children are born imitators . . .

I was often selected as choir-master on these occasions, for I had happened to learn many of the medicine songs and was quite an apt mimic. My grandmother, who was a noted medicine woman of the Turtle lodge, on hearing of these sacrilegious acts (as she called them) warned me that if any of the medicine men should discover them, they would punish me by terribly shriveling my limbs with slow disease.

Occasionally, we also played 'white man'. Our knowledge of the pale-face was limited, but we had learned that he brought goods whenever he came and that our people exchanged furs for his merchandise. We also knew that his complexion was pale, that he had short hair on his head and long hair on his face and that he wore coat, trousers, and hat, and did not patronize blankets in the daytime. This was the picture we had formed of the white man.

So we painted two or three of our number with white clay and put on them birchen hats which we sewed up for the occasion; fastened a piece of fur to their chins for a beard and altered their costumes as much as lay in our power. The white of the birch-bark was made to answer for their white shirts. Their merchandise consisted of sand for sugar, wild beans for coffee, dried leaves for tea, pulverized earth for gun-powder, pebbles for bullets and clear water for the dangerous 'spirit water'. We traded for these goods with skins of squirrels, rabbits and small birds.

When we played 'hunting buffalo' we would send a few good runners off on the open prairie with a supply of meat; then start a few equally swift boys to chase them and capture the food . . .

We loved to play in the water. When we had no ponies, we often had swimming matches of our own and sometimes made rafts with which we crossed lakes and rivers . . .

We had many curious wild pets. There were young foxes, bears, wolves, racoons, fawns, buffalo calves and birds of all kinds, tamed by various boys. My pets were different at different times, but I particularly remember one. I once had a grizzly bear for a pet and so far as he and I were concerned, our relations were charming and very close. But I hardly know whether he made more enemies for me or I for him. It was his habit to treat every boy unmercifully who injured me. He was despised for his conduct in my interest and I was hated on account of his interference.

What Charles Eastman describes are the games by which the boys played themselves into the hard and difficult Indian life through imitation and practice. Our life is different. Nevertheless, the games the children of the miners in the industrial areas of the Saarland were still playing fifty years ago have more similarity to the games of the Indian children than to the dreary boredom which our schoolchildren have to suffer in the cities today. Georg Meilchen, a miner with a good memory, wrote down these games for me. He says:

The best time of our schoolboy life was the autumn holidays. We really had a chance to recover from culture and run wild. We drove the cattle to the fields and were left to our own devices for the rest of the day and lived like Stone Age men. The first thing we did was to make a fire, however hot the sun might be shining, and to build a hut. Then we looked for potatoes in the fields and roasted them in the embers. With our homemade fishing lines we caught fish; people were not so particular about it in those days. We also hunted frogs and ate their legs — fried on a stick like the fish. For vegetables we had sorrel as well as young fir-shoots. We also ate turnips and kohlrabi. We ran increasingly wild.

Sometimes this peaceful life was disturbed by the boys from the neighbouring village who invaded our territory. But we bravely attacked the enemy and forced him to retreat. For long-range weapons we used hazel sticks which we cleft at the top: into the crack we put horse-chestnuts and bombarded the enemy with them. In close-combat we used our whips. We still talked a long time about those fights when we were back in school and the grey normality of everyday life had begun again . . .

The boys of today know neither the whipping-top nor the hoop. They do not know how to make a whistle out of willow bark, or a water-pistol out of elder, or a sling. They do not know how to keep a fire alive during the night: we used dried wood-fungus, since we rarely possessed matches. Neandertal Man will have kept his fire alight in a similar way. Boys of today have no idea what to do with a vaulting pole or a pair of stilts. Neither do they gather the wild stone-fruit any more and put it in the hay to make it soft. . . . We did not do this out of necessity, because all of us had orchards, but then, man's first occupation was that of hunter and gatherer and that still broke through.

We boys had a game which we called Sauball. It was a kind of hockey. A cloth ball, which we had made ourselves, had to be hit into the opposing goal with a stick. Children do not throw sharpened sticks any more. A piece of wood, one foot long and sharpened at both ends, could be hit a long distance through the air with another stick. This must have been an old game, for 'throwing pointed sticks' means in a metaphorical sense to play dirty tricks.

That is just about all I can remember.

It is quite a lot! Plenty of stimulus and a great many possibilities were open to these children, and the limits to their freedom were clearly defined and easily understood in their context, as well as the reason for their existence. The corn and the grass could no longer be cut cleanly where it was trodden down. Nothing was destroyed, there was no senseless going on the rampage — nor were animals cruelly treated. To eat fish and frogs' legs was part of hunting and nourishing oneself. At home chickens and goat-kids were also killed and eaten. Even burning the inside of hollow willows did not kill the tree, but created a shelter. Georg Meilchen told me that only a short while ago, during a downpour, he had taken refuge in a willow which his gang had enlarged with fire.

All those things the children experienced, understood and assimilated through the games that have been described, and also through their participation in the daily and yearly cycles of the countryside, created a broad, solid foundation — made provision for life. What had been grasped through action could later be learnt anew through thought. Or it continued to work in the subconscious and aided the adult to stand his ground in his hard mining job. The social faculties put to use and developed in the life of the group of village youths became fruitful in the exemplary comradeship underground, which forms the basis of the healthy 'working atmosphere' of the pits.

In such ways healthy games form and fortify the human being and enable him to grasp the whole field of his environment through play in the widest sense.

We have surveyed this whole field from without to within, following from chapter to chapter the course of the child's incarnation; we have indicated the separate fields by means of the children's games, which contain and encompass one another like concentric circles or shells. Finally, at the end of this path, we reached the child himself by way of those games that represent the human ego.

The following picture may serve as a clarification:

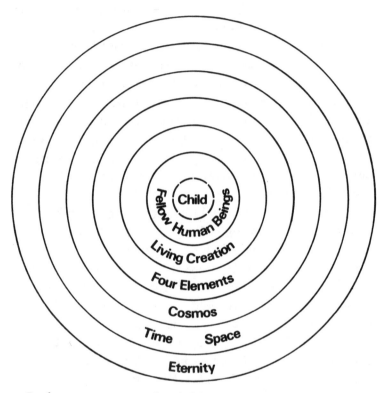

In the centre we see the child, surrounded by the circle of its fellow human beings, who in turn, together with plants and animals, belong to the realm of living creation. These all live on the earth, which the people of past ages believed consisted of the four elements — earth, water, air and fire — in different combinations. As the child comes closer to this view of the ancients in his experience than to that of our modern science, the fourth shell shows the four elements. Our earth belongs to the cosmos, the world of sun, moon, planets and stars, which thus forms the next area. This is still subject to the laws of space and time, which constitute the next shell, and they in turn are embedded in eternity — in the spirit or God, or whatever one may call it.

From without to within, in describing these realms we have traced the children's games related to them. But it is from within to without that the child names its surroundings as it learns to speak. First it says 'Mummy', then 'wow-wow', then 'light' or 'water' or 'car', then 'moon' . . . Only at the end, when it can say nearly everything else, does it call itself 'I'.

The adult has various means at his disposal of coming to terms with the whole range of his environment. For well over half a millenium *experimental research* has become used in more and more areas — including that of the inside of man, and not only of his physical inside! Research has superseded the ancient *magical* methods and — in the meantime — overcome, or at least banned them. *Art* and *philosophy* can lead us through all spheres. But the path of children is and remains that of *play*. Unchanging down the ages and across the world, their games resemble each other. Today a peculiar game is still played in the Caucasus and round the Mediterranean with little bones from sheep or goat feet; recently these bones have also been manufactured from other materials. This game is known from prehistoric finds; it has been able to survive for thousands of years! In surprisingly conservative manner, children also keep hold of certain customs, even when their original meaning has long been lost. The custom has grown into the game of a certain age-group. The *Uffahrtsbrut* (*Himmelfahrtsbraut* or Ascension-Bride), which the children in the area of one small principality carry from house to house decorated with flowers on Ascension Day, is a late descendant of a heathen spring goddess.

Simply by a staircase of games, children have reached the world of adults from time immemorial. Each step is made up of the games of a particular age-group.

It can happen that a child suddenly stops and looks back

to an earlier step with surprise and even wistfulness. 'The young ones *after* us' two sisters used presumptuously to stress when they were around thirteen or fourteen years old. When he was twelve years old, August Winnig had such an experience[20]:

When from the Regenstein I saw the Devil's Wall lying beyond the town, I remembered the time when I had played there. That had been a long time ago, and I felt tempted to visit it once more. On one of the next days I went there. Everything was familiar to me, and yet I felt somewhat strange there. I had the feeling as if this was really all my property, and when I met strange boys there who had now taken over the areas and caves where we used to play, I felt their activities like a breach of my rights.

Thus I also found the old Itschen Cave. I crawled into it and searched it. It seemed to me as if it had not been four years since I left the fellowship of the cave, but as if it were only yesterday that I still belonged to it. Just as in our time, the nooks and crannies were padded with moss and made into seats. At the back, in the same place as with us, was the fire-place; charcoaled twigs and blackened stones indicated where it was. In a big crack, which went far into the rock, the weapons were buried under the loose sand: sharpened sticks, children's bows, arrows made of reeds with a tip fixed on made from the wood of the elderberry bush, an old penknife, a hollow key which had been turned into a pistol by drilling a hole — everything as it had been at the time when I belonged to the membership of the cave.

But I found one thing which we had not owned: a small box with a little bit of fine tobacco left in it and several clay pipes. This was the sign of progress, the only thing which had been added as a pastime since my day.

I sat down on the place which had always been mine, and rested from climbing around. Strange thoughts came to me. I had found the cave unchanged — the same crannies, the same stones with the holes worn by the elements, and the quartz seams, the same cracks as in my time. Just as then, it served as a hide-out for a band of boys who played the same games as we did, and had the same pastimes. Not many years ago we, I, had owned that cave. We had dwelt in it, and had not thought that one day it could be different. Now it belonged to other boys and I was here as a stranger, an intruder, who no longer had any business here.

How many boys of our town might not already have played in this cave? My elder brothers had told me about it, even my father sometimes laughed when the Itschen Cave was mentioned and refreshed some memories of his youth, which had seen him, too, in this cave. Perhaps he had also sat in this place, had looked at the weather-worn holes and had tried to form pictures and figures out of their intricate confusion, which the imagination was always ready to do. And before him? Perhaps our grandfathers and great-grandfathers had already indulged in the games in the cave and in the green crevices of its environs, just like us. And now they had already lain a long time in the churchyard, their grave mounds long since sunken in and surrounded by wild creepers.

Now I was here. But no, my time was also already past. I had also grown out of the years which belonged to this cave. At first I was frightened by this thought. I was but twelve years old, and yet something already to be over and irretrievably lost!

Children resist leaving out steps in their play. One girl in the lower third form was younger than the girls in her class. In the lessons this made no difference. During the breaks, however, she would play her games with the girls of the class below. The break-time conversations of her classmates had no interest for her yet.

And Now?

It has been reserved for our industrial society, where high estimation of the intellect has priority, to put in question and mutilate the ancient and wonderful staircase of children's games. Very questionable substitutes are often put in place of well-tried steps. The first impression is one of impoverishment. Eighty different games, which were certainly generally known among Flemish children at the time, have been discovered in Peter Breughel's painting, 'Children at Play'. How many games do children still have among them today? If one went through the streets and playgrounds to count, one would have a hard job to find eighty.

Our civilization is gradually producing an opposite picture. If we look once more at the image of the spheres surrounding the child, we realize how it becomes more difficult for the children of today to enter them through play.

Who is still able, with inner conviction, to talk to children of their heavenly home? Even fairy-tales which describe spiritual facts in true pictures are demythologized, 'deactivated' and looked upon with suspicion. Even children's right to space for playing is disputed: the streets belong to the traffic, the courtyards to garages, parks rather to dogs than children, flats are too small. And time? People do not have it for children; on the one hand they want to 'save' it, on the other hand to 'spend' it. Even in connection with looking after babies the aim is ever more to save time for the mother — by the use of mechanical devices for rocking the baby and providing it with music! And finally, the period of childhood, of playing, is to be cut short by teaching children to read prematurely.

Moon and stars disappear behind a barrier of luminous advertising. How many children have seen the moon landing on television who are not even acquainted with the different phases of the moon?

Earth makes you dirty, water is wet, a draught causes a cold, and fire burns. Plants are 'poisonous' or 'not allowed', animals 'bite' or are 'nasty'.

Other people are coldly criticized at home, or children have to be warned against them as if they were enemies.

From all sides impressions and stimuli converge on the child — how is it supposed to find 'itself'?

In view of all this, it is not really surprising that defensive reactions, destructive impulses and lack of social behaviour make our young people a problem.

How shamelessly profits are made out of children! It begins with the super, prestige pram. Beautiful and well-proved children's toys disappear from the market because they are not profitable enough. In exclusive craft toy-shops it is possible to buy these once generally available toys; and for some of them it is worthwhile not jibbing at the cost. Instead of these the newest hit or latest rage is put on the market year after year — always something new — but as far as toys are concerned, it is always new children who play with new pleasure with the things that have delighted a particular age group for ages past. But these do not supply 'big business'; Therefore children and parents — especially the latter — are persuaded of ever-growing needs. And when our young people, who were able to *have* everything, but *do* nothing as children, grow up and earn money themselves, is not the adult world, the world of commerce there, ready, like a pack of thieves, to take it away again? First, wishes and desires are artificially aroused by sophisticated methods, and then superfluous, even harmful and dangerous things are boosted and sold as necessities. No, we need not be surprised: our society is hostile to children, so our children are *bound* to become hostile towards society!

Our environment is becoming increasingly sterile and more and more deprived of all possibilities for play. Even our cities used to offer fine opportunities for play. What adventures were to be had in back yards and lofts! Anyone who was a city child in Germany after the last war will remember the ruins with pleasure. That was a world full of adventure, surprise and danger. There were green, secret hide-outs where the ferns grew on the walls, towering remains of walls and sheltered meeting places. It was possible to build, climb and make fires. Only children were at home in the labyrinth of paths which ran through this wilderness. Today, such eyesores have been removed. The eye is regaled by properly looked after house-fronts, well cared for parks and clean, boring playgrounds. Whilst parents live in unprecedented comfort, the children have more toys than their fathers and mothers and grandparents put together. But they have to pay for that by experiencing restrictions unknown to their ancestors.

If one voices the idea that children have come badly off by the exchange, then one only meets incredulity. Should one dare to suggest letting children make something of their own accord — giving them old planks, hammers, nails and saws instead of costly concrete sculptures — then one is considered eccentric, sentimental or foolhardy.

Should there be found, however, the necessary support, financial as well as idealistic, and an adventure playground really comes about, then some of the neighbours will immediately feel themselves sorely disturbed by the happy activity of children and a bit of wood-smoke. The noise of cars and the exhaust gases are gladly borne as the side-effects of industrial progress, but *children,* that goes too far! Children themselves have no possibility of bringing their needs to attention. They have no representatives in parliament and no vote which has to be taken into account. As a social group, therefore, they are bound to come off badly.

The individual can do little against the enormous power which more and more dominates mankind, and causes human beings to do and sanction inhuman things. What can ordinary people in ordinary situations actually do to protect their children against the Moloch of commercialism, which, with no regard for their true being, wants to mould children into average consumers and then exploit them? Where can one start, so that the young people of today, looking back on the games and playthings of their youth, do not just bitterly say: 'Someone must have made a damned good profit on them' — or even worse: 'They bought off their parental responsibility damned cheap that way. They filled my hands and left my heart empty.'

Woe betide them and woe betide us, if not at least *one* memory arises: 'But wait, — wasn't there that wheelbarrow my godfather brought on my fourth birthday — he'd made it himself in his holidays — solid and sturdy, with my name burnt into the side, "so that no one can pinch it" — that was a joy!'

It is up to us to create such joys, to allow wonderful things to happen, which live on in the memory. It does not always require enormous effort — the something special and unforgettable can be very trifling. My grandfather, who knew how much his two granddaughters liked to rummage in his waste-paper basket, took care to 'charge' it

119

specially with pieces of coloured paper and small boxes, so that they could find something nice in it.

The gold thread, the branch of fir, which 'the Christ-child had dropped on the stairs', formed the climax of Christmas delight for a small boy without brothers or sisters. The accumulated anticipated joy streamed from this high point into the celebration of Christmas Eve. In another family such a ceremonial anticipation of joy took place every Easter: going for a walk with Father, on which one always found something 'which the Easter hare had dropped'. This was followed by the Easter egg hunt in the garden. The eldest son was fourteen when he had to take the father's place on these walks and inconspicuously conjure the little chocolate eggs on to the wayside for his smaller brothers and nephews during the walk. It thus became clear to him for the first time how this Easter fun had worked. The reaction was, of course, not disappointment, but thankfulness. The next brother still thought for years that someone had gone ahead in the early morning and prepared the surprise. This Easter walk was at least as important and exciting as the actual hunt in the garden afterwards.

The lead-up to festivals and presents, irradiated by anticipated joy, can have a much stronger effect than the actual festival itself. The element of suspense belongs especially to the toys, the things the child actually sees coming into being. This starts with the piece of bread for supper, which tastes much nicer cut into pieces and running up to the mouth as a 'train'. There is the folded paper cut to make the chains of dancers or little animals that cause such surprise, all the little things made in a few minutes, even if it is only the handkerchief-mouse that makes such sudden leaps.

Bigger things follow: little ships, a waterwheel, and finally, a major object like a rocking horse, a doll's house or even a small house somewhere in the garden, just for the children.

Our 'straw hut', built by Father, was still called that when it had long outlived its second or third cardboard roof. A small stove stands inside, and for over forty years the little house, by now half collapsed, has been the scene of children's happiness. These are memories that soothe: a knitted doll which one saw growing under Grandmother's hands, the fat baby doll one saw come into existence under the knife and needle of one's elder sister, which one always feared was 'for another child' and which was there after all at Christmas in its knitted blue woollen suit! The doll's mother of that time now has five children of her own, but the joyful feelings of that time were seldom matched by any later happiness, and never surpassed.

The relatives of a seriously ill child often try to tempt it back to life with a special toy. In a children's clinic in Heidelberg a small boy suffering from meningitis was lying dangerously ill — the doctors no longer had any hope. The father told the nurses: 'I promised him a sailing ship — I'll build him one now.' The nurses, although convinced that the boy would die, found it good all the same that the distraught father sought 'distraction' through the model-building.

After only a few days, the father brought the beautifully completed ship and stood it at the bedside of his unconscious son, whose life was seeping away. If only that comforts the poor man a little bit, thought the nurses. The next morning the 'dying' child opened its eyes and said in a tone of satisfied recognition: 'Well, there is even my sailing ship!' — and recovered.

Occurrences like the kite-flying day of the two American farming families, performances, it does not need to be anything so very extraordinary — *at the right moment* a quite simple event can become a highlight of the first magnitude and achieve things of decisive importance in the child. To know at every moment what is *now* the right thing, what is *now* important — that is the desire of the teacher, that is his aim.

For such games, such toys, created for a particular child or particular children at a particular moment, are the allies of all good and constructive forces. The children do not feel themselves as mass-beings, stamped with an umpteen-millionth of the mass-price of the mass-product in their unimportance and barterability, but they experience their uniqueness as personalities! Something special was created for just these children and later they will take their own responsibility seriously. They will lead their lives, not as mass-particles which let themselves be driven, but as human beings whose thoughts and actions are of consequence.

Notes

[1] Harlacher, Richard, *Lernen im Spiel* [Learning through play] Katz-mann, Tübingen, 1967.

[2] Steiner, Rudolf, *The Education of the Child*, Steiner, London, 1965.

[3] Carossa, Hans, *Eine Kindheit* [Childhood] Insel, Frankfurt a.M.

[4] Andres, Stefan, *Der Knabe am Brunnen* [The boy at the well] Piper, Munich.

[5] Fowler, Frances, 'The Day We Flew the Kites', *Reader's Digest*, August 1949.

[6] Foerster, Karl, *Garten als Zauberschlüssel* [Garden as magic key] Rowohlt, Reinbeck, 1934.

[7] Steffens, Lincoln, *The Autobiography of Lincoln Steffens*, Harcourt, Brace, New York, and Harrap, London 1931.

[8] Lucas, Margie, 'Jetzt spielen wir Bonanza' [Let's play cowboys] *Saarbrückner Zeitung*, August 1969.

[9] Kügelgen, Wilhelm von, *Jugenderinnerungen eines alten Mannes* [An old man's memories of youth] Langewiesche-Brand, Ebenhausen.

[10] Ssoulchin, Wladimir, *Ein Tropfen Tau* [A drop of dew] Pustet, Munich.

[11] Viebig, Clara, *Das Miseräbelchen* [The little wretch] Wiesbadener Volksbücher.

[12] Lusseyran, Jacques, *And There was Light*, Little, Brown, Boston 1963 and Heinemann, London 1964.

[13] Christaller, Helene, *Als Mutter ein Kind war* [When mother was a child] Reinhardt, Basel, 1933.

[14] Gallico, Paul, *Love of Seven Dolls*, Joseph, London, and Doubleday, New York, 1954.

[15] Melchers, Maria, *Kirchstrasse 22*, Grünewald, Mainz.

[16] Donnell, Annie Hamilton, *Rebecca Mary*, Harper, New York, and Hodder & Stoughton, London 1906.

[17] *Erziehungskunst* [Journal of Rudolf Steiner Education] Freies Geis-tesleben, Stuttgart, 5/6 1969 and 3/4 1968.

[18] Saint-Exupéry, Antoine de, *Citadelle*, Paris, 1948 (The extract quoted in this book is not contained in the abridged translation, *The Wisdom of the Sands*, Harcourt, Brace, New York, 1950.)

[19] Eastman, Charles, *Indian Boyhood*, New York, 1902 (Dover, New York, 1971).

[20] Winnig, August, *Frührot* [Red of dawn] Wittig, Hamburg.

Resources for the Kindergarten and Home

Most of the firms listed will send free catalogs or samples although some do have a small fee. Some suppliers only carry a few items suitable for Waldorf-oriented play.

Simple Toys to Encourage Play

Apple Garden
P.O. Box 2666
Napa, CA 94558
(800) 600-8921

Handmade toys, books, kits, etc.

Back to Basics Toys
2707 Pittman Drive
Silver Spring, MD 20910
(800) 356-5360

Large selection of toys including craft supplies, dollhouses, games, and vehicles.

Camphill Village Products
Chrysler Pond Road
Copake, NY 12516

Dolls, climbing bears, rattles, and other natural toys.

Dollies & Co.
860 Inca Pkwy.
Boulder, CO 80303
(303) 499-2611

ECO Trading, Inc.
21218 Street Andrews Blvd.
Suite 123
Boca Raton, FL 33433
(800) ECO-1131
(407) 852-7364
Fax (407) 852-8155

Imported wooden toys, push toys, clothes racks, etc.

Elves and Angels
P.O. Box 70
Wytopitlock, ME 04497-0070
(207) 456-7575

Wooden toys.

Emily's Toy Box
P.O. Box 48
Altamont, NY 12009
(518) 861-6719

Wooden toys, Ravensburger games and puzzles, cooperative games, etc.

Family Pastimes
RR 4
Perth, ONT K7H 3C6
Canada

Cooperative games.

Handworks
Route 1, Box 138
Afton, VA 22920
(703) 456-6596

Basic kits for sewing, knitting, and other activities for children.

Hearthsong
156 N. Main Street
Sebastopol, CA 95472
(800) 325-2502

Toys, crafts, beeswax.

Heartwood Arts
Wooden Toys
15 Tri Brook Road
Hillsdale, NY 12529-5935
(800) 488-9469

Wooden castles and knights, gnome houses, and people.

Magic Cabin Dolls
P.O. Box 64
Viroqua, WI 54665
(608) 637-2735

Dolls, toys, props for play.

Marvelous Toy Works
RR 1, Box 124A
Stillwater, PA 17878
(717) 925-5708

Wooden cars, wagons, rocking horses, toys, and games.

Meadowbrook
Herb Garden
Route 138
Wyoming, RI 02898
(401) 539-7603

Herbs, beeswax, toys.

Meadow View Imports
81 Kingstown Road
Box 407
Wyoming, RI 02898

Ostheimer wooden toys.

Natural Baby Co.
816 Silvia Street, 800 B-S
Trenton, NJ 08628-3299
(609)771-9233/(800)388-BABY

Soft dolls, wooden toys, games, as well as clothes for baby and Moms, diapers, and accessories.

Nova, Inc.
817 Chestnut Ridge Road
Chestnut Ridge, NY 10977
(914) 426-3757

Dolls, toys, games, art supplies and wholesale supplies for kindergartens.

Once Upon a Time
P.O. Box 6023, Station 1
Pompano Beach, FL 33060
(305) 785-4371

Handmade dolls, toys, looms, craft kits, cradles.

A Real Doll
P.O. Box 1044
Sebastopol, CA 95473

Doll and toy kits, cotton knits, supplies.

Real Goods
966 Mazzoni Street
Ukiah, CA 95482
(800) 762-7325

Energy-sensible technologies.

Root Children
505 Jarvis Street
Whitehorse, Yukon, Y1A 2H7
Canada
(403) 667-2411
Fax (403) 668-6101

Handcrafted Brazilian, native, and dollhouse dolls, gnomes, and fairies.

Seventh Generation
1 Mill Street
Box A-26
Burlington, VT 05401
(800) 456-1177

Ecological household goods.

Shining Light Baby Co.
P.O. Box 2036
N. Babylon, NY 11703-0036
(516) 243-1944

Wide assortment of child safety products, puzzles, homeopathic remedies, Weleda products.

Sweet Pea Natural Toys and Gifts
3338 N. Southport
Chicago, IL 60657
(312) 281-4426

Truth's Dolls
P.O. Box 42
Fulton, CA 95439
(707) 984-8749

Handmade, soft-sculptured dolls with natural materials.

Turtle Moon
P.O. Box 161
Bodega, CA 94922
(707) 829-6732

Natural fiber dolls, silks, costumes, kits, play frames, and supplies.

Vidar Goods
P.O. Box 41
Faber, VA 22938
(804) 263-8895

Woodpecker toys, Camphill toys and crafts, Black Dragon (Celtic) crafts, and anthroposophical prints and cards.

World Wide Games
Colchester, CT 06415
(860) 537-2325

Toys and puzzles for older children and adults.

Children's Furniture and Wooden Toys

Ron Brecher Designs
294 Hungry Hollow Road
Chestnut Ridge, NY 10977
(914) 426-0638

Wooden benches, tables, playstands, furniture; builds any furniture upon request.

Casey's Wood Products
15 ½ School Street
Freeport, ME 04032
(207) 865-3244

Wood turnings, dowels, dishes, little people, and more.

Catino and Co.
611 Mountain View Avenue
Petaluma, CA 94952

Chairs, dollhouses, tables, hutches, cubbies made to order.

Community Playthings
Route 213
Rifton, NY 12471
(914) 658-3141

Sturdily-made furniture, toys.

Kaplan Companies
1310 Lewisville-Clemmons Road
Lewisville, NC 27023
(800) 334-2014

School supplies and furniture.

Craft and Toy-making Supplies

Aetna Felt
2401 W. Emaus Avenue
Allentown, PA 18103
(800) 526-4451
100% wool felt.

June Albright
RR 1, Box 123A
E. Thetford, VT 05043
(802) 649-8717

Plant-dyed silks and wool felt, silk flower fairies.

Bartlettyarns
P.O. Box 36
Harmony, ME 04942-0036
(207) 683-2251

Wool yarns, roving, blankets, yarn accessories.

**Briggs and Little
Woolen Mills**
Harvey Station,
New Brunswick E0H 1H0
Canada

Carolin J. Brooks
59 Clarence Street
Strathroy, ON N7G 1H2
Canada
100% wool felt, wooden craft
materials, doll and toy kits.

Central Shippee, Inc.
P.O. Box 135
Bloomingdale, NJ 07403
Felt in 100% wool and wool
blends.

Chaselle Inc.
9645 Gerwig Lane
Columbia, MD 21046
(301) 381-9611
Art and craft supplies for
schools, including colored tissue paper.

A Child's Dream
P.O. Box 1499
Boulder, CO 80306
(303) 442-0437
100% wool felt, cotton knit, wool
fleece, mohair yarn, silk, toys.

Clems and Clems
650 San Pablos Avenue
Pinole, CA 94564
(510) 724-2036
Fine wool.

**Del Mar, Knorr Beeswax
Products, Inc.**
14906 Via de la Valle
Del Mar, CA 95014
Sheets of colored beeswax,
beeswax candles, and ornaments from molds.

Flying Colors
RR 1, Box 123A
E. Thetford, VT 05043
(802) 649-8717
Plant-dyed silk, wool felt, beeswax candles, and flower fairies; wholesale to Waldorf
schools and stores.

Mountain Sunrise
Peggy Smith
279 Swanzey Lake Road
West Swanzey, NH 03469
(603) 357-9622
Plant-dyed wool fleece, 100%
wool felt and yarn.

Rupert, Gibbon & Spider
P.O. Box 425
Healdsburg, CA 95448
(800) 442-0455
Silk, dyes, and craft kits.

Sarah's Silks
131 Third Street
Windsor, CA 95492
(707) 836-0679
Silk processed with natural and
low-impact dyes, rainbow silks.

Wholesale to schools and stores.

Walter Kelley Co.
3107 Elizabethtown Road
P.O. Box 240
Clarkson, KY 42726
(502) 242-2012

Beeswax by the pound in blocks or strips; also bee-keeping supplies.

Sureway Trading Co.
826 Pine Avenue
Suites 5 & 6
Niagara Falls, NY 14301
(416) 596-1877

Variety of silks in white and colors.

Textile Reproductions
Edmund and Kathleen Smith
Box 48
W. Chesterfield, MA 01084
(413) 296-4437

Plant-dyed unspun wool, yarn, cloth, thread, and felt; sewing supplies.

West Earl Woolen Mill
130 Cocalico Creek Road
Ephrata, PA 17522
(717) 859-2241

Wool batts for quilts and stuffing toys (no catalog).

Wool Works
Box 27
Shawville, Quebec J0X 2Y0
Canada
(819) 647-3749

Thick 100% wool felt, wool yarn, roving, batting, and knit clothing.

WoodsEdge Wools
P.O. Box 275
Stockton, NJ 08559
(609) 397-2212

Unspun silk, wool, alpaca, cashmere, mohair, and merino.

Waldorf Education

Association of Waldorf Schools in North America
3911 Bannister Road
Fair Oaks, CA 95628
(916) 961-0927

Waldorf Kindergarten Association of North America
9500 Brunett Road
Silver Spring, MD 20901
(301) 460-6287

Suggested Reading

Publishers

AWSNA   Association of Waldorf Schools of North America, 3911 Bannister Rd., Fair Oaks, CA 95628, (916) 961-0927.

AP   Anthroposophic Press, RR 4, Box 94A1, Hudson, NY 12534, (518) 851-2054, Fax (518) 851-2047.

FL   Floris, 15 Harrison Gardens, Edinburgh EH11 1SH, U.K.

MP   Mercury Press, 241 Hungry Hollow Rd., Spring Valley, NY 10977, (914) 425-9357.

RSC   Rudolf Steiner College Bookstore, 9200 Fair Oaks Blvd., Fair Oaks, CA 95628, (916) 961-8729, Fax (916) 961-3032.

RSP   c/o Biblios, Star Rd., Partridge Green, Horsham, W. Sussex RH13 8LD, U.K.

SSF   Steiner Schools Fellowship, Kidbrooke Place, Forest Row, Sussex, RH18 5JB, U.K.

WKA   Waldorf Kindergarten Association, 1359 Alderton Lane, Silver Spring, MD 20906, (301) 460-6287.

OP   Out of Print.

(Many books can be borrowed from the Rudolf Steiner Library, RD2, Box 215, Ghent, NY 12075.)

Selected Lectures and Writings by Rudolf Steiner

"The Education of the Child in the Light of Anthroposophy," 1909, AP and RSC. Short introduction to Waldorf education and child development.

"The Kingdom of Childhood," 7 lectures in Torquay, England, August 1924, AP and RSC. Child development and Waldorf education. Includes the incarnation process, child as a sense organ, imitation, development of fantasy, the kindergarten, as well as teaching main lessons, numbers, plants, and animals.

"The Poetry and Meaning of Fairy Tales," 2 lectures, Berlin, December 1908 and February 1913, MP.

"Practical Advice to Teachers," 14 lectures accompanying the "Study of Man," AP and RSC. Teaching the various subjects of the Waldorf School curriculum, including work with the temperaments, the art of teaching with imagination, and practical advice to the first Waldorf School teachers.

Prayers for Mothers and Children, AP.

"Soul, Economy and Waldorf Education," 16 lectures, Dornach, Christmas 1921–22, AP and RSC. Lectures on phases of child development, health and illness, and aesthetic, physical, religious, and moral education. Includes "The Child Before the Seventh Year" and "Knowledge of Man as a Basis for Education."

Child Development and Health

Wolfgang Goebel and Michaela Glöckler, *A Guide to Child Health*, AP.

A. C. Harwood, *The Recovery of Man in Childhood*, AP and RSC, and *The Way of the Child*, AP.

Karl König, M.D., *Brothers and Sisters: A Study in Child Psychology*, AP and RSC; *The First Three Years of the Child*, AP.

Bernard Lievegoed, *Phases of Childhood*, AP and RSC.

Joan Salter, *The Incarnating Child*, AP.

Daniel Udo do Haes, *The Young Child: Creative Living with 2–4 Year Olds*, AP.

Caroline von Heydebrand, *Childhood: A Study of the Growing Soul,* AP and RSC.

Practical and Philosophical Aspects of Waldorf Early Childhood Education

Rahima Baldwin, *You Are Your Child's First Teacher,* AP and RSC.

Brigitte Barz, *Festivals with Children,* Gryphon House.

Thomas Berger, *The Christmas Craft Book,* RSC, and *The Harvest Craft Book,* AP and RSC.

Thomas and Petra Berger, *The Easter Craft Book,* AP and RSC.

Diana Carey and Judy Large, *Festivals, Family and Food,* AP and RSC, and *Celebrating Festivals Around the World,* AP.

Gudrun Davy and Bons Voors, eds. *Lifeways: Working with Family Questions,* AP and RSC.

Finger Plays, Fifty-two finger plays, MP.

Elizabeth Grunelius, *Early Childhood Education and the Waldorf School Plan,* RSC.

I. Haller, *How Children Play,* AP.

Rita Jacobs, *Music for Young Children,* AP.

Freya Jaffke, *Toymaking with Children,* AP and RSC, and *Advent for Children,* OP.

Julius Knierim, *Quintenlieder, Introduction to the Mood of the Fifth,* RSC.

Elisabeth Lebret, *Pentatonic Songs,* OP.

Friedel Lenz, *Celebrating the Festivals with Young Children,* AP.

Nancy Mellon, *Storytelling and the Art of Imagination,* RSC.

Rudolf Meyer, *The Wisdom of the Fairytales,* AP and RSC.

Brunhild Müller, *Painting with Children,* AP and RSC.

Karin Neuschutz, *The Doll Book: Soft Dolls and Creative Play,* OP.

Carol Petrash, *Earthways: Simple Environmental Activities for Young Children,* AP and RSC.

Sunnhild Reinckens, *Making Dolls,* AP.

Johanna Russ, *Clump-a Dump and Snickle-Snack,* pentatonic songbook, MP.

Susan Smith, *Echoes of a Dream,* artistic activities for young children, RSC.

Michaela Strauss, *Understanding Children's Drawings*, AP.

M. van Leeuwen and J. Moeskops, *The Nature Corner*, AP and RSC.

Kindergarten Association of North America, Volume I: An Overview of the Waldorf Kindergarten, and Vol. II: A Deeper Understanding of the Waldorf Kindergarten. Collected newsletter articles, WKA.

Kundry Willwerth, *Let's Dance and Sing, Story Games for Children*, MP.

Wynstones Kindergarten, *Summer, Autumn, Winter, Spring, Spindrift, Gateways*. Collections of songs, stories, and verses from the British kindergartens, RSC.

Bronja Zahlingen, *Plays for Puppets and Marionettes*, WKA.

Elementary and Secondary Waldorf Education

Education as an Art, with "The Child at Play" and "The Child When He Paints" by Caroline von Heydebrand, "The Needs of Young Children" by Nora von Baditz, and "Education and the Science of the Spirit" by Rudolf Steiner, AP.

Dotty Turner Coplen, *Parenting a Path Through Childhood*, AP.

Francis Edmunds, *Rudolf Steiner Education: The Waldorf School*, RSC, and *Renewing Education*, AP and RSC.

Sue Fitzjohn, et al., *Festivals Together: A Guide to Multi-Cultural Celebration*, AP and RSC.

Brien Masters, *A Round of Rounds, The Waldorf Song Book* and *The Second Waldorf Song Book*, AP.

Rene Querido, *Creativity in Education*, RSC.

Roy Wilkinson, *Curriculum of the Rudolf Steiner School: Questions and Answers on Rudolf Steiner*, RSC.

Isabel Wyatt, *The Seven-Year-Old Wonder Book*, RSC.

Other Books of Interest

David Elkind, *The Hurried Child* and *Mis-Education: Preschoolers at Risk*, RSC.

Jane Healy, *Endangered Minds: Why Our Children Don't Think*, Simon and Schuster, and *Your Child's Growing Mind, A Guide to Learning*, Doubleday.

Martin Large, *Who's Bringing Them Up? Television and Child Development*, AP and RSC.

Jerry Mander, *Four Reasons for the Elimination of Television*, RSC.

Pantheon Edition of Grimms' Fairytales, with introduction by Padraic Colum, RSC.

Joseph Chilton Pearce, *Magical Child: Rediscovering Nature's Plan for Our Children*, Bantam, *Magical Child Matures*, Dutton, *The Crack in the Cosmic Egg: Challenging Constructs of Mind and Reality*, Julian Press, *Bond of Power*, Dutton, and *Evolution's End: Claiming the Potential of Our Intelligence*, Harper.

Marie Winn, *Children without Childhood*, OP, *The Plug-In Drug*, RSC, and *Unplugging the Plug-In Drug*, Viking Penguin.

Journals

The Peridot
921 SW Depot Avenue
Gainesville, FL 32601
Journal of Waldorf ideas.

Renewal
AWSNA
3911 Bannister Road
Fair Oaks, CA 95628
(916) 961-0927
Illustrated magazine of the Waldorf Schools in North America.

Waldorf Kindergarten Newsletter
1359 Alderton Lane
Silver Spring, MD 20906
(301) 460-6287
Newsletter, articles on the importance of play and list of Waldorf schools and other information sheets.

Celebrating the Great Mother

A Handbook of Earth-Honoring Activities for Parents and Children

Cait Johnson and Maura D. Shaw

The enjoyable activities included in this book will help you bring your children into the rituals celebrating seasonal cycles and the sacred days of our ancestors.

"Deeply satisfying. Buy this book and make its teachings a healing part of your daily life." **Brooke Medicine Eagle**

ISBN 0-89281-550-7 • 14.95 illustrated paperback

Birth Without Violence

The Book That Revolutionized the Way We Bring Our Children into the World

Frederick Leboyer, M.D.

As important today as when it was first published in 1975, this ~lassic text has encouraged a generation of parents and birth attendants to consider birth from the infant's point of view. Examining alternatives to the technocentric approach to childbirth, Dr. Leboyer shows how we can create an atmosphere of tranquillity in which to welcome our children, easing the newborn's transition from the peace of its mother's body to the tumult and activity of the world.

"One of the twenty books that changed the world." **Utne Reader**

ISBN 0-89281-545-0 • $14.95 illustrated paperback

Gentle Birth Choices

A Guide to Making Informed Decisions about Birthing Centers, Birth Attendants, Water Birth, Home Birth, and Hospital Birth

Barbara Harper, R.N.

In this book, you will find a new model of maternity care that relies less on high-tech medical intervention and more on personal choice. Parents will find information on the many options available for a safe, meaningful, family-centered birth, and birth attendants will appreciate its value as a resource and teaching tool. And everyone will enjoy the sensitive images of acclaimed photographer Suzanne Arms, that capture the joy and intensity of the birth experience.

"Exactly the sort of guide that pregnant women have been needing to help them sort through the myriad number of choices and options which confront them in the Nineties."

Robbie E. Davis-Floyd

ISBN 0-89281-480-2 • $16.95 illustrated paperback

The Child of Your Dreams

Approaching Conception and Pregnancy with Inner Peace and Reverence for Life

Laura Archera Huxley and Piero Ferrucci

Exploring the frequently neglected psychological and spiritual dimensions of conception, childbirth, and parenthood, the authors show how you can positively influence the mental and emotional development of your unborn child, and create the greatest possible potential for his or her future.

ISBN 0-89281-365-2 • $12.95 illustrated paperback